# Me a

# By Sarah Parker Foster

Donna Tanner
506A Laurel Lake Rd
Salemburg, NC 28385

*Jamie Garrison*

Text copyright © 2015 Sarah Parker Foster

All rights reserved.

# Contents

# Preface

I cannot believe it is happening to ME. I just cannot fucking believe it. Why does it have to be me? I have waited so long for someone to write about how distinctly it sucks. I have wished someone would tell the whole story of how it tears families apart from the very beginning. People need to know that Huntington's disease isn't just a diagnosis, it is a life fuck. And not just for the person who has HD. For everyone around them.

So I decided I to write about it, as my brain deteriorates. I will share every detail with you here so you'll have some clue, when I am no longer able to talk, what I have been through. And how I thought I was having a normal life until HD made me turn my lizard head around and spit black venom all over my past life. It is now all black as hell. My whole life, from

when I was a baby, is contaminated by HD.

And this is how it began.

# How you can live with Huntington's disease

It wasn't always as easy as it is now. You cried a lot when you found out you had Huntington's disease (HD), and wouldn't leave the bedroom. HD is a rare neurodegenerative disorder, but it doesn't seem rare. Neurodegenerative means brain wasting. As we speak, and probably long before you knew it was happening, proteins are clogging up your brain matter and causing it to die.

Why I have not killed myself

HD starts before doctors officially proclaim you have it. They reserve that proclamation for when you begin to have uncontrollable writhing, dancelike movements called chorea. My point is that by that time, the disease has already torn your brain to bits.

You can't remember things, you get depressed, and maybe try to kill yourself, or if not, you think about it a whole lot more than other people. You think about how much easier it would be for the people you cared about if they did not have to deal with disintegrating you: day after day of crises, emotional outbursts, apathy, and perseveration.

Like I was saying, the executive functioning part of your brain turns to crap and to begin with, you can't organize things or follow simple routines. You can't do two things at once, or hear what someone is saying to you unless you give them your full attention. First you have trouble following recipes, then you have trouble bathing yourself, you totally are unable to regulate your emotions and your personality changes into something unrecognizable. You say mean things to people you care about. You talk like you're drunk until you lose your ability to speak altogether. Then you just sit there, or lie there, unable to do anything, including communicating your wants, needs and feelings (which you continue to have), until you die of aspiration, starvation, or your heart gives out. Somewhere during this process, your body begins to writhe, in most cases, and your movements can become so severe that your body burns off all of its fat to try to keep up. You die of starvation.

You dance yourself to death.

But instead of simply killing yourself, you find a use for your life. You learn by accident that you gain strength by describing your weaknesses. You blog and explain your troubles and fears. People say you've helped them understand themselves or their loved ones. You feel happy about that, so you keep blogging and then you see what else you can do to help other people who have HD. You try to make their lives not suck. It makes you feel better because their happiness is yours. You learn to love your life, despite HD,

because you now can connect and support other

people. You grow emotional muscles by shouldering

the burden of other people's HD. You love yourself

again. You are living your life to its fullest expression,

like a assuming a full lotus.  You know you will still

dance yourself to death.

But your dance will be a showstopper.

# Two of the longest, most excruciating weeks of my life.

Time crept by, and I was painfully aware of my position in the middle of a pendulum about to stop. Where it stopped might change my life forever. But, more than anything, I wanted to know what the rest of my life would be like, whether I should plan for Elderhostel trips all over the world in my eighties or decide whether or not to use a feeding tube to prolong my life.

# The fun stops here

Not really. But what do you expect from a book about how Huntington's Disease is impacting my life and the lives of those I care about? You don't get a lolly pop. This is not a feel-good movie.

This is about a genetic screw-up that has been called "the worst disease in the world." That's because it takes its time killing your brain, cell by cell. It destroys your family tree like a fungus. The people that care about you suddenly have to care FOR you, and the you they are caring for is someone they ultimately don't recognize.

HD is not a mixture of Parkinson's, Alzheimer's, and ALS, with a dash of schizophrenia. It is its own monster.

My own monster. Is it yours too?

I'm going to tell you about my tale of self-destruction. A play-by-play.

I will not always have my happy face on.

I dare you to come back.

# At odds with the odds

Results day did not go as planned. My psychiatrist at the time was unreliable, and he, in true form, dropped the ball the day I was to receive my results. I was supposed to have a mental health professional with me when I got the results of my DNA test by phone but he went AWOL. Dr. Derr, my medical doctor, filled in at the last minute. Randy and I went into her office. It was Christmas Eve.

The phone call from the geneticist came and they said that before they gave the results to the patient, it was routine for them to tell the health professional first, so Dr. Derr left the room for a while and came back in. I couldn't read her face. I agonized over the results for every second of the past two weeks. But here in the room with Dr. Derr, about to pick up the phone, I knew this was something that was all in my head, I was just having a nervous breakdown. I'm a hypochondriac. It was with this in mind that I answered the phone call from Chapel Hill.

"Sarah," the voice said, "I'm afraid that the results weren't what we had hoped." And I collapsed and the rest was really a blur. They told me my CAG was 40, and the lower the CAG the later it sometimes manifested in people. I remember Dr. Derr being so supportive. I remember Randy holding me up and getting me home and putting me to bed, where I alternated between wailing and being catatonic. It was the worst thing that could possibly happen and my life was over.

The odds were not in my favor. I have never won anything in my life, not even a church raffle. Why did I, in the doctor's office, think I had a special, secret relationship with luck that was just going to spare me from this catastrophe?

Yet today I am playing the odds once again. I have begun participation in the CREST-E trial. The trial is to see whether high-dose Creatine can slow the progressive functional decline that affects people with HD.

"You either have the placebo or the drug, one or the other," said the coordinator as she handed me the packets, and I found myself at odds with the odds again. If fate dealt me a placebo then I will have no good effects from the study drug.

With my track record, I bet I have that placebo.

Someone suggested that I skip the study and just take a therapeutic dose of Creatine anyway. There is already evidence to support its use and many people with HD are already taking it in the hopes of slowing things down.

But sometimes (I tell myself) the most important thing is playing the odds. Getting tested to break free from secrecy and unknowing. Doing a drug trial to be a small part of large conclusions.

I'm either right or wrong about this.

# Robin Williams in early stages of Parkinson's: Looming, inevitable HD

August 14, 2014

Ever since I tested positive for Huntington's Disease, I have felt it looming inevitably over my life.

All of my dreams and plans for the future became null and void.

Instead of going on Alaskan cruises, I will spend my golden years deciding whether or not I should use a feeding tube to prolong my life.

That's the thing about HD, It's coming and it's not going to be pretty as it arrives and devours.

I always, always, carry this in the back of my mind, even on my very best days.

It's not surprising that suicide rates are higher for people with HD. I didn't think that I would be approved for testing because I was borderline suicidal at the very thought of being positive. But I was desperate to know, to put a name to whatever was invading my mind, Somehow I convinced them to draw the blood and send it off. But after I tested positive, I didn't see any point to anything anymore. It would take me a year to come out of a deep depression and a couple more years before I could resume a somewhat limited daily routine.

And all the while it is coming. With every stagger and slurred sentence it announces itself. And I have learned to simultaneously acknowledge and ignore it, to strike a balance I can live with. I accept a crappy future while I live each day fully.

There was also the sense that I let everyone down by testing positive. I ripped away my family's happy ending. I came to understand that it was the disease doing the dirty work, not me. But I can't help but wonder about Robin Williams and whether he thought he would be letting the whole entire world down because he was sick.

That burden might be too heavy to bear.

Today I know who I am and I'm not afraid.

# Blissfully unaware

August 15, 2014

Not realizing that you have HD symptoms is actually a sign of HD. Many people don't realize they have chorea or are acting abnormally in any way. That's one reason it often goes undiagnosed.

When my mom's foot started writhing, I asked my dad if he noticed it and he said, "Yes, but I'll never say a word about it to your mother." She remained unaware of the involuntary movements for years.

As mama's disease progressed, she became paranoid and thought the water supply was poisoned. She called several local agencies repeatedly to report the poisoned water, and the confusion she must have felt was the opening that finally enabled my brother to convince her to go to UNC-Chapel Hill for an evaluation.

My mom's diagnosis of Huntington's Disease was based on her presentation and family history. She refused to give a blood sample for DNA testing. She insisted that hell no she did not have Huntington's Disease. Several doctors told her repeatedly that they were sure it was true, but they were unable to convince her. Surprisingly, she actually agreed to take some medicine that would lessen her severe chorea.

I told my mom I was going to get tested for HD and several months later, she asked me the results of my test.

"Mama," I said, "are you sure you want to know? Do you know what it could mean?"

She said yes, so I told her that I tested positive and that is how my mom became aware that she has HD. When we talk, she says, "How's yours?" I will let her know what symptoms I have and then I say, "How's yours?"

She always says, "I'm weak. Tired. Weak, weak, weak." My mother just turned 80. She certainly must be tired. She has been fighting an epic battle. In my family, HD takes its time.

Part of me hopes that by the time my hard symptoms hit, I will lose my awareness. The notion of living through HD and being fully aware of it seems horrific, like enduring a surgery that lasts for 25 years without anesthesia. Perhaps the lack of awareness is a blessing.

But if I was somehow able to face the thing with my eyes wide open, it might make the road easier for my caregivers. I might be more compliant, more reasonable. I would certainly be more like me. If there is such a thing as an awareness muscle, I am exercising it now in the hopes that I can stick around and notice the ride. I am discussing symptoms as they occur and planning to have frank discussions as things unfold. I am developing simple signs to use with my loved ones. One means "I love you." The other means "I'm still in here."

I hope I will be.

# Forgetting Ferguson

August 16, 2014

My short term auditory memory has been destroyed. My neurologist says it is because HD has damaged my brain. Given a list of five words, I can't repeat them.

Last night, a Facebook post mentioned members of the media not being allowed to go somewhere. I asked my husband what could possibly be going on that would lead to such a situation. He told me that he had explained in great detail the entire situation down in Ferguson to me earlier that morning. I have no memory of the conversation, but I believe him. I often forget entire conversations. I began asking questions about it. Normally, he would have filled me in without missing a beat, but it was late and he was tired. He suggested I Google it. I thought this was a reasonable suggestion so I did so this morning.

Reading about the situation in Ferguson has made it stick in my brain longer. Images like print and pictures don't fade away as quickly as sound does. For the same reason, I prefer texting and emailing my friends instead of talking to them so I can remember the information and have a record to refer to if I still forget what they have told me.

Social situations are awkward because I never remember people's names and I often strike up conversations with people that I come to realize we've already had.  Since moving to New Bern, I've attended events each year which have pretty much the same guest list. After five years, I still ask the same introductory small talk questions, like "Do you have kids?" Meanwhile, other people know everything about me because they remember our previous conversations. It feels odd, frustrating and embarrassing. I imagine that I seem normal to people until they get past the "Hello."

I have started skipping a lot of those events and spending time instead with people who have stayed on the merry-go-round long enough for me to retain basic details about their lives. These friends are willing to patiently and repeatedly answer the same questions. They understand my disability.

There's no way I can forget them.

# I'm perseverating. Again.

September 3, 2014

If you thought I was well, you were wrong, because HD is insidiously infiltrating my life. But I am doing much better than a lot of other people so I want to do everything I can to raise awareness about the hell that we and our families inhabit.

One of the symptoms of HD that I exhibit (if you haven't guessed by now) is perseveration. I will fixate on an idea and my mind just keeps going back to it, no matter what. This causes problems if I continue to dwell on a negative event or situation. Recently my psychiatrist, my husband and I talked about how to best handle it. She said that at this point we have some control over it but that later there was a good chance that I would need medication to control it. We talked about strategies that my husband can use to redirect or distract me when I perseverate about something bad.

But for now, she suggests that I use my power for good instead of evil.

I could choose to perseverate about having this wretched disease and be miserable. I have done that many times and it only creates more gloom and despair. Instead I am choosing to happily perseverate about the HD Pie in the Face challenge.

The first day of the challenge, my husband immediately sensed what was going down, and we set some ground rules. Family comes first. The challenge comes second. I still need to take time to be a wife and mommy. I've only felt uncomfortable a few times, like I wanted to run, screaming, from the dinner table and turn on my computer. And I'll admit that sometimes I've woken up in the middle of the night and come downstairs to work on the challenge.

For the time being, I've found something safe and productive to go round and round about and it satisfies that urge. Scratches that itch.

On the other hand, my perseveration about James Franco taking the HD Pie in the Face challenge, I've come to realize, is borderline creepy. Just because he retweeted a tweet doesn't mean he is obligated to be the poster boy for HD. That is magical thinking. But I've still been pushing for this idea to become a reality, despite feeling uncomfortable about being rude and invasive. Tweeting him regularly to politely invite him to take the challenge is a fairly benign interaction between celebrity and fan. And I encourage anyone who wants to continue tweeting him. But for me, it's starting to feel wrong because *my*expectations for the outcome aren't totally realistic.

Today I got an email from James Franco's publicist saying that they had all the information about the challenge and if James decides to do it then it will be on his own.

What does the possibility of a "No" do for my perseveration? It throws me for a loop because I have done all that I can do that I feel comfortable doing. Like things aren't going the way I've planned for them to go and now I'm at a loss. Never mind that there are a million other celebrities that might agree to take a pie. In my vision of how this was going to play out, Franco was going to take a pie, then the challenge would go viral. But he has 2.4 million other Twitter followers and I have to introduce myself to the reality that we will succeed without his help.

So I've decided, with the help of my husband, to stop perseverating about James Franco because I don't think it serves me, Franco or the HD community well.

Today, instead, I wrote up a press release about the HD Pie in the Face Challenge and sent it off to about 15 major news outlets. And guess who was not mentioned at all? I'll call that progress.

Now that I've pointed my compass in a different direction, I am even more certain that we'll find success by doing what we've been doing. So I hope you'll keep throwing pies and making challenges until we're viral.

I certainly will!

# On being sick and having HD

September 11, 2014

Whenever I contract a minor illness, I have to pay special attention, especially to the boundaries of the illness.

I have a chest cold now, and the last few days I've spent mainly in bed. Typically around day two, depression will swirl by as an effect of my inactivity and can blend itself so subtly with my minor illness that I can't sort symptom from depression. If I don't make it a point to separate the two, depression delays my recovery time. I could be in bed for days with a minor illness that most people would walk around with.

Another reason for my increased time in bed is that I can't multi-task well anymore. When I am sick, I can only do that. Bits of my daily routine that were already formidable become mountains I don't have the strength to cross.

Then there's the part of me at some point during the illness that says, "Dammit, haven't I been given enough? Do I have to deal with this, too?" I have to remind myself that many people with HD face other, serious illnesses, like cancer, and I should chill out about my little chest cold.

Once I finally proclaim myself well, and try to go back to practicing my daily living skills, it's as if I'd never formed them as habits before the illness. It takes me weeks, with help from my therapist and husband, to get back into my "regular" daily routine.

So here's hoping that I won't catch anything else anytime soon.

Hope you're healthy, too.

# If I could be cured

September 18, 2014

Gene Veritas succinctly and superbly announced the Phase 1 Trials for a drug that could stop or even reverse Huntington's Disease.

He understands and can explain it better than I ever could. You can read about it at his blog:

http://curehd.blogspot.com/2014/09/moving-toward-potential-treatment-isis.html

For a month, I've had mainly pies on my mind. The last couple of days I've spent at the beach, crossing a few items off my bucket list.

Now that I am home, and Gene's announcement is settling in my brain, do I dare to dream that I could be cured? That none of my children will ever endure HD? I am thinking about what my life would be like and how I would change as a person. If I was cured, I would:

- Stop second-guessing my body's every move, safe in the knowledge that I am healthy.

- Skip being sad after each visit with my boys, knowing that the mom they see next visit will not have deteriorated as a result of HD.
- Lift the enormous weight of guilt because my husband will not have to spend another day as my caregiver. I am sure he will feel commensurate relief and gratitude.
- Not explain myself to anyone any longer. I'll be able to say what I mean, feel the appropriate feelings at the correct intensity, and move fluidly and gracefully, like a fish through water.

- Stop eating like there is no tomorrow and take better care of a body that I am not angry at anymore.

- Go off disability and work full time doing something I enjoy.

- Plan to be an elderly tourist with my elderly husband, middle-aged sons, and dozens of grand daughters in foreign lands.

- Invest myself more emotionally in other people's lives, because I know HD won't steal me from them.

- Make sure that everybody that can be cured, gets cured.

Are you allowing yourself to wonder? To dream? To hope?

I'll admit, I haven't for a long time until now.

**Gene Veritas, is it safe to dream yet?**

# When a good day's not good.

September 22, 2014

Today could have been worse.

I can't say that it has been a bad day. On a bad day, I cry and despair at my lot in life and stay under the covers. I used to have nothing but bad days and question what I'm even doing here.

So it could have been worse.

It just wasn't great. I woke up with a sense of foreboding doom that hovered over me all day. I was slightly productive, which was good, but soon productivity gave way to tiredness.

I napped.

When I woke up, I wasn't refreshed. I felt the same dark cloud, as if it had been waiting by the bed, resume its station over my head.

But now today is almost over and I made it through. I didn't experience joy or many of the positive emotions on the spectrum. But I know there's a pretty good chance that tomorrow will be better, especially if I get plenty of sleep tonight.

Sometimes living with HD is a matter of managing to get through a day without allowing it to become awful. Cocooning, to hide from the bad things that can happen. Avoiding any emotional interactions. Given that criteria, today was a success.

See you tomorrow.

# Stressing with HD

September 25, 2014

I'm not liking it.

But it's inevitable that life includes stressful moments, incidents, and even periods of prolonged stress.

Since January I have been in a period of prolonged stress, with a month's respite thrown in.

I have a problem that I perseverate about. It never, ever leaves my thoughts, no matter how many pies are thrown. I look at it from every angle and try to solve it. I fear the worst, and then the worst actually happens and I am not sure if I can handle another moment.

I know I am living in the problem and not the solution, but I have attempted several solutions that I expected to solve the problem, but they did not.

So now it feels like I'm drowning, or worse, constantly on the verge of drowning. It permeates my dreams. It is in the back of my mind during every conversation I am having.

It's sucking the optimism out of my soul.0

## Sleeping through the bad parts

October 2, 2014

I am having a love affair with sleep right now. Napping, night time sleep, and that delicious second sleep after I put my son on the bus.

Previously I've mentioned that I am in a prolonged stressful situation. Sleep has become my respite. I don't stay in bed all day, but if I feel like I'm getting overwhelmed, I'll set my alarm for 60 to 90 minutes and fall asleep to the sound of my regular, slow breathing.

I've found napping to be more effective than taking that half of a klonapin that would put me to sleep anyway. I wake up and it takes a while for the stress to find me again. It eventually does, but for the time that I am sleeping, and those moments just after I get up, I feel calm and oblivious to my concerns.

I am taking two or three short naps a day and look forward to bedtime like a child on Christmas Eve.

The old normal was making myself stay awake all day, until I learned that naps are good (the new normal).

I regret missing out on all those naps

# I can cook dinner

October 10, 2014

After a recent family discussion, during which I lamented the fact that I do nothing to contribute to the household, my 9 year-old son said, "You do something, Mom. You cook dinner."

I agreed with him that I do usually make dinner.

His father washes our son's clothes and puts them away. He also cleans our bathroom, bedrooms, kitchen, cars and walks our German Shepherd Dog. He does these things after he comes home from working a day which is invariably interrupted by a stream of calls and texts from me, asking about something I've forgotten, or having emotional moment, or perseverating about something.

Then on the weekends, he keeps the children entertained and active while tackling household projects and tending to whatever needs I exhibit. He mows the grass and lays out brick walkways in our yard. He takes care of injured squirrels and disposes of snakes.

He is fastidiously clean and keeps his surroundings and his personal items neat and orderly.

He listens to me when I cry through a depression or seethe through an angry moment. He holds me when I feel myself slipping away from the real world. He suggests gently that I do things which might make me feel better, like exercise and outings. He never lets me blame myself when I feel I've screwed up. He always contradicts me when I put myself down.

Our house has the hugest front door I've ever seen and he could have walked out of it a million times and never come back.

But that's the one thing that he hasn't done.

I think I'll make an extra special dinner tonight.

# In the body of a stranger

October 16, 2014

Things are going on that I don't like.

Not one bit.

When I speak, I use the synonyms of the words I want to choose. When I type I can find the right words just fine, but I have to use a full size keyboard. My fingers are not agile enough to thumb type.

Taking the groceries out of the cart and putting them on the conveyor belt is a challenge. There is too much going on. The people at the grocery store help me take the food out of the cart and put it back in once it has been scanned.

I perseverated on a breathing pattern I didn't like and then couldn't stop it and wound up at Urgent Care, hyperventilating.

I have fears about the Ebola virus which are not rooted in fact, I specifically fear that people with Ebola are going to try to get in my house. I know this is an unlikely scenario, but it keeps playing in my head and I am sad that I think thoughts that aren't normal.

When I think about cutting or handling raw chicken, I want to vomit. I am concerned that my hands will stay contaminated no matter how thoroughly I wash them.

Reluctantly, I will sit somewhere other than the spot I have rooted myself for the past three months.

The daily routine is getting harder and my husband has to urge me to do the things I am supposed to do.

And finally, when I am in bed preparing to sleep, I feel my hips and my legs, moving without me.

Together, it feels like I am being dragged around in the body of a stranger and I am struggling to keep up.

And I don't like it at all.

# On brain death and dying

November 3, 2014

I can sense that part of my brain has given way to the clumps of proteins. There are new things that I can't do. My ability to remember text that I have just read is deteriorating. I can look up on the computer in the living room how to clean my cook top and by the time I've gotten to the kitchen, I've forgotten how. I've tried this ten times in a row and failed. I am going to write it down on a piece of paper and take the paper into the kitchen with me. This idea just came to me, but it is an obvious solution.

I find myself just standing, staring aimlessly, while my husband looks at me, wondering if I'm about to do something or want to do something and am lost. Usually it is one of the two.

This morning I was sitting on the couch and I told him that the couch needed to be moved to the right. He waited, while I sat there, then instructed me to get up, walk to the other side of the couch and push it. I felt relieved after I had done it, but I hadn't connected a task needing to be done to the steps it takes me to do it. My husband does that more and more for me now. If I say I have a headache he says to get up, go upstairs, get the Tylenol, take it and come back. If he did not direct me, I would just sit around and complain about my headache as it worsened.

Words are splattering out of my mouth in false starts, words related to the ones I want, but not synonyms. For example I might say "Boston bomber" instead of "Boston baked beans."

I am glad that I am aware of what is happening and that my husband is so good at helping me.

I read about the girl with brain cancer who chose the day she died and I respect a person's right to do that.

But I don't think I would have the courage. I could see myself, in a moment of despair, impulsively taking my own life, but I couldn't put Christmas presents for everyone in the attic, and deliberately go about planning the event of my death. I don't want my kids to see me deteriorating, but that is not enough impetus to make me plan my own death. I respect that others feel differently and marvel at their courage.

My mother has HD and is able to find something to be happy about each day, even if it is just a piece of food. I would rather her enjoy that piece of food and live than die so I would not have to see her as she is. She is a lot nicer now that she is on medication, and if she had chosen to die to spare my horrors, I would have never seen that part of her.

I have a friend who is dying of brain cancer and his wife bought an adjustable bed for two and put it right in front of the fireplace, so they could enjoy the fire together until he dies.

Everyone's journey is different and that some paths to death are more horrifying and terrible than others. Even in the HD community, how and when it hits you and the suffering that is causes is varies wildly.

I count myself among the lucky, so far.

# Trying on a new hat

November 8, 2014

The other night, I had a house full of non-family members. This was a huge deal for me because I prefer the comfort of being home, with just my family, or occasionally a single visitor. I spent two days cleaning my cook top, and another day cleaning the rest of the downstairs of the house. I even took off the sheet of plastic that covers the tablecloth.

When they came I was happy, because my guests are all friends who I love. I felt a tolerable sort of nakedness as each person stepped through the doorway, but soon I relaxed. We sat around talking about things like gratitude and achieving our dreams and nobody even saw the cook top. I talked about my anxiety about whether or not I could buy my house.

Someone asked me how I would feel if it was a done deal and I owned the house.

"Marvelous!" I said.

"So just feel that way," my friend replied. And I tried on the feeling and liked it, so I am trying to stay with that feeling.

Now the house sits around me, silently, like it has been unfaithful but dares me to challenge it. I see the signs. The water spilled on the couch. The chairs moved from one room to another. But now I love it all the more for providing a safe place for me to see the very friends it enfolded.

Yesterday one of those friends from the other night called me. She heard the conversation of the feelings switcheroo about the house go down.

"Sarah," she said. "What if you applied this to your HD?"

She explained that if I acted as if I was well, then some part of me would have to fall in line, at least the emotional part. And HD, by its very nature, can surely conjure up emotions. Then there are all the secondary emotions produced by the first line of emotions... If learning to act "as if I was well" spared me and my family even one instance of this turmoil, then it would be worth it the act. If trying on the hat of someone well causes me to keep it together when I want to explode, because explosions are not congruent with my new vision of myself, then pass the hat.

Do I think that having the mindset that I am well will cause my DNA to change and spare me from Huntington's Disease?

No.

Do I think it could delay progression?

Maybe. Who can say? And why not live in the light rather than the darkness?

The only problem is, while it was so easy to conjure the joy of having the house, I'm having trouble doing the same with HD. I need a clearer vision of what not having HD would look like.

Maybe I can start each day by greeting myself with, "Hey, today I am healthy!" A relatively true statement that puts me on the right track.

We'll see how it goes.

# Do not mess with me today

November 11, 2014

My teeth are clenched. I've taken the extra klonapin and I am still seething. I can only give short responses to my 9 year old. Just the basic info. He asked why I was talking to him that way and I didn't tell him it was so I wouldn't explode. I told him it was because I need to just get the main information out right now.

Heaven forbid someone should need a ride or a meal or anything I don't want to do which is everything except stay in front of my computer screen.

I wasn't like this when I woke up. I was all "act as if I don't have HD." Something, I don't know what, triggered my emotional pressure cooker and now I can't control it. I can only clench my teeth so I won't say anything I will regret. When I get into emotional places this bad I sometimes try to take a nap to reset myself. Sometimes it helps. I am headed there now.

But first I wanted to describe the searing, powerful anger that I feel which is directed towards nobody. I don't think anyone would characterize me as an angry person, and I hope that this is not a taste of things to come, or I really will be angry.

Thanks for listening.

# Can't get it out of my head

November 14, 2014

There is something that I am worrying about and thinking about and waiting to happen and I told myself that a blog entry would be, if not an effective distraction, a way to describe what is going on in my head.

There is a loop that connects me to the thought. I do things, like write this, to try to make the loop larger, so I won't think about the thought as often. But I get agitated when that happens and I have to let myself focus on the thought for a minute until I calm down. I work it into every conversation. It is my inner monologue. Even just thinking about writing about it makes me feel a little closer to it, a little more comfortable. But now I am no longer distracting myself, I am drugging myself with the deliciously irritating closeness of the idea. And there are 24 more days to worry and think and wait, to the exclusion of all else. I am too stressed to engage in any sort of functional activity, leaving even more time to perseverate.

I can't not worry about it and I can't not think about it. If I stop thinking about it, then something bad might happen, but something bad might happen anyway. I know it makes no sense.

This exercise has served as no distraction. In fact, it has redoubled my connection with the thought by putting it into roundabout words and allowing me to have this whole new layer of vague vocabulary I can think about when I'm pretending not to think about what I shouldn't be thinking about.

Curses! Foiled again.

# The littlest boy

November 17, 2014

The littlest boy is now nine and stands up to meet my chin. He grows quickly as I decline slowly.

He has known I've had HD almost as long as I have. He understands that he and his two big brothers are at risk, but knows that there are lots of possible treatments that will come about by the time he needs to start thinking about HD in his own life.

He was born with the gift of intuition. He can read my emotions before I can identify them.
He carries bags up stairs for me and waits for me to catch up. When he asks me a question, he gives me time to answer instead of asking another person instead.

More times that I can count, he has watched my husband lead me, sobbing uncontrollably, to bed or to the therapist. I try to blubber at him to not worry, that I'll be OK.

Other times when I tell him I need some time alone, he goes. I've told him that I have to give myself time outs sometimes to cool off. But those times I do lose my temper, he is quick to forgive me and tell me he loves me.

We talk about HD a lot. He asks a lot of questions and I give him honest answers (including the silver lining of an impending cure.) We know about hdyo.org.

He expresses more interest and warmth towards me than I can express to him, and, sadly, he is used to the imbalance.

But I never let too many moments pass without telling my littlest boy that I love him.

# HD and the holidays

November 26, 2014

Of course HD is riding my back as I once again gallop into the season of rituals. This year, however, we are making some changes due to some of my limitations.

I am not cooking a big turkey dinner and all the side dishes for Thanksgiving (which is tomorrow here in the US.) I have cooked the bird and everything else for years, including last year. But this year, I can't envision myself planning and orchestrating the feast. Part of it may be growing apathy towards daily tasks. But I can't deny that my organizational skills in the kitchen have declined substantially in the past year. I regularly require help preparing simple, daily meals for the family. I often burn myself and have trouble pouring things, opening things, and taking things out of the oven.

I still had to brave the crowds at my grocery store (which cruelly rearranged its items recently) but I came out of there without too much emotional fallout. One of the employees put all of my merchandise on the conveyor belt for me, and I was very grateful, because often I get tangled up in the process of doing that and a line of people builds behind me.

I usually always use a list, but I decided that ignoring the crowds *and* paying attention to the list would take up all of my mental energy, so I just winged it, and looked around at what was there.

My husband suggested that this year we have something fun, but easy to cook, so I don't have to be in the kitchen all day. I **immediately** agreed and suggested that we have Mexican food. None of the kids like traditional Thanksgiving food anyway and we end up throwing most of it out.

When my husband gets home from work, he is going to make salsa. We might even begin our Mexican meal at dinner tonight and just carry it over throughout tomorrow. When we have Mexican food, I put all the components on the buffet table and everyone builds their own meal. I don't have to worry about who doesn't like what. Everyone will like something.

I also bought some cocoa, mini marshmallows and candy canes (which I am going to crush and put in the hot cocoa) for the boys. I saw characters on a TV show enjoying this drink and thought it would be a simple way to make someone happy.

Maybe I'll have one, too.

# How selfish am I?

December 2, 2014

I've been thinking lately about how HD has enhanced my self-centeredness. I feel an unwanted, unfolding apathy blanketing things that are going on around me. Maybe it's a defense mechanism because I wouldn't remember events anyway. Maybe it's the apathy that grows along with HD.

External happenings fall away around me, abandoning me to my own concerns, desires and fears. What I want seems so painfully important that I can almost feel it out loud. But picking up on someone else's experience is like leaning in to listen to a nearly inaudible whisper.

There are major life events going on in the lives of the people who I care about. I wish I could respond to their situations in the ways that I used to: long conversations, active listening (where I listened to them), visiting, or even just sitting with another person's pain so they won't feel so alone. Instead it feels like I'm plundering through what's still liveable of my life at the expense of other people's emotional fulfillment.

But if I can't see it, feel it or want it, then I have a hard time recognizing, comprehending and responding in a normal way. What is out of my realm reminds me of static on an old TV.

And of course, even concentrating and writing about this topic adds another layer of selfishness.

To live with myself, perhaps I should avoid characterizing my decline as selfishness. It's part of the life HD has dealt me. And I'm already missing the people I love because of it. I feel connections, relationships and memories slipping away. I am sad because I know it's going to get a lot worse and there's nothing I can do about unless I could muster up an extroverted, empathetic, enthusiastic me.

Oh, I would if I could.

# "It" equals everything

December 9, 2014

I do **it** wrong.

I don't do **it** at all.

I don't do **it** completely.

I don't remember how to do **it** anymore.

I forget to do **it**.

I've already done **it** and have forgotten that I did **it**.

I hurt myself trying to do **it**.

I dread doing **it**.

I don't want people to see me try to do **it**.

I don't want to do **it**.

I wish I didn't have to do **it**.

I won't do **it** today.

I won't do **it** until I have to.

I won't do **it** until someone tells me I have to.

I still won't do **it** when someone tells me I have to.

I won't have the energy to do **it**.

I'm too upset to do **it**.

I can do **it** on another day but not this day.

I wish I had done **it**.

I missed out on **it**.

I used to enjoy doing **it**.

I passed up my last opportunity to do **it**.

Is this all there is to **it**?

# How to get my attention

December 16, 2014

I've been initiating fewer spoken conversations lately, because mustering up the energy it takes to gather all the words I want to come out of my mouth makes it seem not worth the effort. So I am being more and more selective about what I bring up.

When you begin to talk to me, chances are I'll be thinking about something else, so I won't hear the first part of what you say. It will take me a few seconds to realize you're talking to me. By this time you're already expecting me to answer but I have not yet understood anything you've said. So I will say something like "Really" or if it's a question I'll say, "Say it again."

While I am working on forming my answer to your earlier question, you might make a follow-up remark. Then I'll either have to stop forming my answer and listen or ignore you and keep forming my answer.

If we are around a lot of people who are talking it is worse, because the din of their words competes for my attention as well. If we are doing something together, like walking, when we are talking, it is harder for me to carry on a satisfying conversation. If I am doing something alone, like cooking or taking medications, I am liable to make mistakes in what I'm doing if I listen and talk to people.

The best way to make sure I'm engaged from the start is to first make eye contact with me and say, "Sarah" then count to yourself one-Mississippi, two-Mississippi and wait until you see my face "turn on" before you speak. That will give me time to interrupt what I was thinking about and then focus on what you will say.

Sitting behind me and expecting to have a conversation with me is neither successful nor pleasant for me. Since I am sitting forward, I am paying attention to what is in front of me, like my breakfast. I can't tune in to a voice behind me while I am looking in front of me, and I feel lost and a little scared, like things are being announced to me, instead of having two way communication.

Let me know you understand what I need by coming over to where I am and sitting so our eyes will meet.

Because it's only going to get worse, and I want you to know my concerns and wishes about how you should interact with me while I can express myself through the written word.

# Getting out of a sinkhole

December 19, 2014

Last night I was at the bottom of the abyss and a sinkhole formed and I clung to the walls of the abyss so I wouldn't be sucked down into oblivion. It was so emotionally real that it felt geographically real. This was my condition until sleep redirected me, through a series of related nightmares, to this morning.

I wondered, as I woke up, how I could still be alive. My insides felt bruised and torn. My skin, like an exoskeleton. It took all of my resolve to get up and go to the bathroom.

"Don't forget," said my husband, who had been awake for some time, "you have a meeting at 9:30."

"Go for me!" I wailed. He had known about my slip into the abyss. There have been plenty of visits to the abyss before, so many that the darkness knows my name. But my husband had no idea about the sinkhole. I was unable to verbalize the extent of this new emotional horror I experienced the night before.

Instead I stood, paralyzed.

"You need to get up and restart your routine. Now get ready."

My eyes shot daggers at him as I pulled a hat over my unwashed hair and looked for my shoes. I was furious with him for not doing what I needed. I only gave in because the meeting was to plan a fundraiser for an HD non-profit. The only thing greater than my stubbornness, anger and despair was my desire to see this HD event through. I had no idea how I was going to make it through the meeting without crumpling into a babbling heap. So, yes, if it had been anything else, even a mental health intervention, I would've returned to the fetal position in my bed.

I sort of brushed my teeth and went downstairs to find my husband dressed and ready.

"I won't go instead of you," he said, "but I'll go with you."

And that's all it took. No more hopelessness, or misplaced anger. Instead: peace.

He wasn't going to make me go through it alone.

I've never loved him more than I did at that moment.

And that's how I got out of the sinkhole. I wasn't pulled out.

Randy came in and we climbed out together.

# What's my line?

January 3, 2015

I've mentioned that my oral communication skills are declining and that it is easier to convey ideas through the typed word than the spoken word.

Sometimes I will have a couple of false starts when speaking. I will sputter a few words, take a deep breath, and then try to pronounce the words that are waiting to come out.

Word retrieval is also a problem. My family is very patient with me, providing me with the silent time I need to find the right word.

But lately, I've grown impatient with myself and have started asking for help finishing my sentences. I'll say, "what's the word?" if I don't have a clue as to what the word is, and they will offer up some suggestions.

Sometimes I'll name something that has things in common with the word that I want to say. Yesterday, I said, "the chiropractor's office" when I wanted to say "the physical therapist's office" and that gave them a big enough clue, along with the context of the rest of my sentence, to figure out what I meant.

Lately this fill in the blank exercise with my family feels like a game show, with everyone competing to answer correctly and quickly, as if motivated by a timer. Other times, it reminds me of call and response rituals at church. Sometimes, when we're all at a loss as to what I am trying to say, we just come up with silly answers and make a joke out of it.

And why not have fun, if an opportunity arises? This is not a funny disease, but I am learning that humor is a great strategy to cope with daily challenges.

And we all have constant, unlimited access to laughter.

# Walking between raindrops

January 14, 2015

It is a sad constant in the HD Facebook community, but the past few days have nearly torn my heart out. It seems like every post I read is raw with pain, fear and loss. People not knowing what to expect from their own bodies. Other people watching their loved ones spiral away to someone forever different. These are people I know and care about through our mutual support system, and my heart breaks for them today.

On one hand I feel some sort of survivor's gift because I've remained functional while I've witnessed other people's swift declines. I've been blessed to be able to walk between raindrops, to dodge the effects of the damage being done to my brain. But then again, I have an urgency that never abates. The knowledge that one day when I don't expect it and am not prepared for it, the rain is going to pour down on me and wash the me away.

I'm not ready.

# Groundhog Day

February 2, 2015

I haven't written here for awhile because I've been working on a writing project for someone. It took me the better part of the month to do it. I wasted days perseverating, researching tangential information that was superfluous to the project. But the perseveration came in handy in the big picture. It has been like wearing Mule blinders. My whole focus has been on the project. Nothing else all day, every day. When I finally released it yesterday, I felt lost and confused. I was happy to have the stress of the project behind me, but I have emerged from a controlled state of being. Like the Groundhog, I have popped out of my hole.

Over the past month, I have noticed that my writing skills are slipping. I am having difficulty spelling ordinary words, like "except" and find myself pondering for several seconds the spellings of words that used to flow automatically out of my fingers.

Yesterday I sat with my family and tried to get a sense of how I have been functioning lately. Both my husband and my son said that I say "Hey" a lot, as a conversation starter or greeting, then say it moments later, forgetting that I already said it. Last night, my son monitored a period in which I said it at least 10 times in five minutes Maybe this is the result of having been focused on one thing for so long and is my way reintegrating myself to having verbal conversations and it will taper off. But I don't know how long I've been doing it. I do know when I speak, my words are mangled and many times I use odd synonyms or words that rhyme instead of the word I am trying to say. I recall that some of my word choices have been funny, but since I did not write them down, I've forgotten them.

I am frequently surprised by bits of new (to me) information my husband shares with me, which he insists that he has already told me. It is hard for me to believe that I could forget so much. But I trust him completely, and know that this must be the way it is.

I have been experiencing slight gyrating movements each night as I wait for sleep to come. Not severe enough to blame on anything but nervous energy.Until last week. We were in bed watching television and my body started making strong movements without my intention or permission. I just lay there for a moment and watched it, then I told my husband, who suggested that I change positions. I did and the movements subsided. Tears streamed down my face and I said, "It's happening, isn't it? I don't want it to start."

I fear the shadow of what is to come and want to go back into my Groundhog hole.

But if I do, I might miss a wonderful spring.

# Valley Girl

February 4, 2015

I know what I am going to do as soon as I post this, so don't be alarmed. I am fully aware that the experience I am about to describe is being caused by HD, and despite how real it feels, it is not reality. After I post this, I am going to go to bed and do deep breathing exercises until I fall asleep. When I wake up, most likely the reset button will have been pressed and I will feel better. If not, I will call my therapist.

But I want to describe what it is like to be down in the valley while I am here. All of the pain from every hurt I've ever felt conglomerates and places itself at the center of my attention. It is an emotional pain so strong that it is physical, it feels like the insides of my head are being scrubbed with steel wool. My mind is flooded with the pain of a hundred horrible memories. Every bad move or misfortune has come back to my attention. The collection of people I love (who don't understand me and are either thinking I have massive character flaws or that I don't give a damn about my family or the world) surround me, I recall them, pointing out my failures as a mother, a person, and even a person living with HD. Then they turn their backs on me. I am alone and the only person who understands is Randy because he has watched HD slither its way in. And he is on a business trip. Otherwise, we would have nipped this in the bud sooner and there would be no blog entry.

I question the importance of my existence and wonder if it would be better if I was gone. If the people I loved would be happier, or achieve the moral superiority they crave, in a world without me in it. I imagine how much worse the people I love will view me as I decline, and I don't want to hate or be hated by my relatives.

The only reason I know I am going to live is because I am absolutely convinced that what I am experiencing is not true, although is seems to be.

It is the lowest of the low. I wanted to try to put it to words, but don't know that I've succeeded.

I do know that now it is time for me to go take care of myself, according to the plan I described above.

So know, as I do, that this will pass and I will be OK. Don't send the police over to check on me.

And don't call me because I will be asleep.

This is something that HD is doing to my brain and I've figured that much out and am lucid.

You'll hear from me later.

# My life as an emoticon

February 5, 2015

So, I'm back, as I assured you that I would be, but today is treating me badly.

Not "I don't wanna live" badly, but I am having a weep-a-thon.

I fear that my dreams for the furture are unrealistic and will not come true. I am afraid that my life's function is going to be mornings of emoting base ugly emotions, like despair, regret, and guilt.

And, later in the day: anger, frustration, and more regret.

My thought processes are not clear. I am stuck in a loop of emotions. I don't know if such a thing as a typical, ordinary day is in store for me again.

Everything people say to me is confusing and I forget it and have to ask over and over. I feel a heavy, heavy weight when I think of the conversations I want to have with my teenage sons, things they don't want to hear or know. It is important that I properly express my love for them before it is too late.

I am going to take another nap.

# Boxing myself in

February 6, 2015

Growing up, our family was allowed to use only one grocery store. Only one hamburger shop.

One drug store. That's because my mom hated the people at all the other businesses in town. Before I knew my mom had HD, I chalked it up her meanness. But later I realized that HD was making her box herself in, shrinking the world she interacted with. The root of it, I figured, was still her intense anger. To me, her anger has always been a thing unto itself: a ball of rage that she could throw anywhere at any time. Until yesterday, I never considered that her anger could stem from her inability to interact with other people.

Yesterday

I went to the pharmacy where my doctor had already electronically sent my prescription. Eager to get antibiotics into my system, my heart sunk when I saw all of the people in line.

I stood in line waiting, the whole time worrying about how the transaction was going to play out when it was my turn. Were they going to understand me when I pronounced my name? Would I remember my date of birth? Would I be able to find the debit card?

By the time it was my turn, I was stressing out about a l lot of things at once. I asked for my prescription and the clerk said that it had not been called in yet. Air raid sirens went off in my head! This is not the way was supposed to play out!  I insisted that it had been sent in. The people in the line behind me were getting restless. I asked the clerk to check.

The clerk walked past the pharmacists, talked to another clerk who appeared to just be coming on duty, then returned and repeated that it hadn't been called in yet and that I should go to the next window. I didn't think she checked at all! I thought she pretended to check to get me out of the way!

I looked at the next next window. It was closed.

I said, "Aren't you going to help me figure out why

you don't have it?" My voice had a cross, unfamiliar

tone to it and I wished I could go back and say it nicer

and smile. But she still pointed to the next window.

I slid down there, but wasn't sure what I was

supposed to do. Was I supposed to wait for someone

to help me? Was I supposed to try to call the doctor?

Were *they* trying to call the doctor? Or were they just

shoving me aside because they thought I was being

rude to them and they were going to teach me a

lesson?

I stood at the next window for 15 minutes and

watched as the clerk helped one person after another.

None of them had any problems with their

transactions. None of them got sent to the

next window. The longer I stood there, the more

frantic and lost I felt. And those feelings

spawned irritability and anger. The situation was

unreasonable, I thought. I could stand here forever,

as if I were waiting for Godot, **because I did not**

**know what action needed to happen to make the**

**situation move forward.**

Trying to pull it together, I called my doctor's

office, but that started another series of

complications.  There was no direct line to the Urgent

Care department where I had been seen so I was put

on hold over and over. At last the receptionist came

back on the line and said she could take a message

and give it to them, because they were really busy.

"This is an emergency!" My cheeks felt hot

because I knew that everyone there (who was not an

employee) was staring at me. I must have freaked out

the receptionist who answered the phone, because

she told me she was going to run over to the Urgent Care building, which was quite a long distance. I stood there, at the next window, on hold, until she returned and instructed me hang up and call back in one minute. I didn't understand why she wanted me to do this and she had to explain loudly and repeatedly that by this time, the regular office was closing and the phones would switch over to Urgent Care.

Urgent Care answered and confirmed that they had called my prescription in. "Will you PLEASE tell that to the pharmacist right here?" I bitterly spat out the words and poked my phone in the direction of the pharmacist. He recoiled. "I don't do cell phones. Put in on speaker." How much harder is it going to be?

I did, and he asked Urgent Care what my name was, looked me up in the computer and stated, without looking at me, that my order was in the midst of being processed. So I went and sat in a corner and waited. By this time I was crying. Thirty minutes later, my order was ready and when I had to enter my telephone number in the machine, I couldn't remember what it was.

The same lady that sent me to "the next window" checked me out and before I left, she said, "I hope you feel better." I wanted to rip out her fingernails. Did she not know that she and her coworkers were the reason I was in this state?

On my way out, I passed an employee and impulsively announced that I had a complaint. The assistant manager, a sweet, innocent young lady, listened as I blubbered about how nice my other pharmacy had been and that the people at this pharmacy weren't nice to me. I told her I was thinking about changing back to my old pharmacy. She apologized and asked if there was anything she could do for me and I said, "No, I just need to go home."

My nine-year-old son had been with me the entire time. When we were safely in the car, I started crying harder. "Nobody else had problems," I said. "They don't understand that it is hard for me because it doesn't look like anything is wrong with me. Maybe if I had worn a sign that told them I was sick, they would have treated me differently and maybe I wouldn't have gotten so upset. They would have known I wasn't a normal person."

"There is 'no normal person', Mom," my son gently said. I stopped crying and told him those were the nicest words I had heard all day.

Back at home, my husband was already up to speed, because I had been angrily texting him a play-by-play. When I told him I might change pharmacies, he pointed out that if I started eliminating the places where I faced challenges from my life, my world would become really small.

He was the one who made the connection.

"You know how your mom boxed herself in with local businesses? Maybe she did or said things that embarrassed her at those places and was ashamed to go back. Or maybe the people at those businesses weren't sure how to handle her behavior because they didn't know she had HD and then your mom got mad at them for not understanding what she needed."

It was an "Aha!" moment. Now I have a better understanding of why my mom boxed herself in.

Now its my turn. How big will I let my world be? While I still have insight, I will try to anticipate and make accommodations to meet the challenges

that surely lie ahead.

But I do not want to build a box of my own.

# Dean Smith, dementia and death: observations of an amoeba

February 8, 2015

If you're familiar with American college basketball, you know that UNC Coach Dean Smith died on Saturday. He was a living legacy and now leaves behind thousands of people whose lives were influenced by his integrity, his advancement of racial equality, and the connections that he inspired among players, their families, and innumerable fans.

But in the years before his death, Smith slipped into the world of dementia. His wife described his condition as "a neurocognitive disorder with multiple etiologies." He exhibited symptoms of Alzheimer's, Parkinson's, vascular dementia as well as the normal toll of aging.

Smith's once famously precise memory was erased. His family wasn't sure what he could and could not comprehend. It is very likely that he forgot about his legendary achievements. His last days were spent silently and unresponsively.

But the good news is that everyone **will remember** and celebrate his wonderful life. Nobody will dwell on the dementia that stole his brain. Coach Smith's condition stole a smaller slice of his life than is the case with Huntington's Disease. His condition will rightfully and forever be eclipsed by the enormity of his contribution to the world.

Now, I'm an **amoeba** compared to Dean Smith in terms of life's accomplishments, and I know of several friends who think I am not qualified to speak of him, because I'm not the perfect fan, the precise statistician, or the master historian.

But I reluctantly compare our lives because we do share a similar end game.

I wonder what people will remember about me? By the time I'd settled down, had a family and spotted a flicker of wisdom on the horizon, HD woke up and started its job. Now it is taking away everything I've built, slowly but certainly, like ants moving grains of sand.

Will people remember my original personality, the things I've tried to do right or tried to make right? The love I've tried to express? Or will they remember a haunted, unreachable, and possibly cruel, stranger who will linger for years to come?

My family and I wonder as well what memories I'll hang onto in the years leading to my death.

From what I know about Smith, he approached life in a way that was never about him.

I, on the other hand, am self-centered, transfixed on the disease and its inevitable destruction of me and my family.

But, inspired by the greatest role model, I hope to use the days ahead to deepen my connections with my husband, family, friends and the HD community.

# Getting my affairs in order

February 10, 2015

After I told my therapist about some things that I have done and want to do, she pointed out that I am getting my affairs in order while I can still function.

Written communication has stopped being easy. Now I have trouble retrieving the words I want and trouble spelling frequently used words. I get tangled up in sentences in a way that I've never experienced.

The loss of writing skills for me is more profound than my already damaged oral communication skills. I know that not writing will alienate me from the world. It will slam the door on self expression.

So I am highly motivated to set forth into words the following, while I still can:

- Tips my family can use to interpret and deal with my symptoms and behaviors. (I see the humor in this)

- A document describing my end of life wishes.

- Letters to each of my three sons describing how "doing the best I could" as a parent varied with every day; how the love I feel for them is unconditional; and how sorry I am that they are at risk.

- A journal of my experience with HD for my family to keep.

- A very personal letter to my husband, that I get teary even thinking about.

Because the task is an acknowledgement of my fate, I'm dreading it . And I know I'll cry a lot and be depressed while I'm doing it. But putting this off isn't a good idea. I can feel myself changing, becoming dimmer, flatter and dumber. Getting my affairs in

order is a process I should wrap up soon.


Because if I wait too long my window will shut

forever.

# Diving into doomsday documents

February 12, 2015

I'm coming up for air here.

A few days ago, I wrote that it was probably time to get my affairs in order while I was still able. "My affairs" include advance directives, a will, my treatment preferences, how to best deal with me, organ donor information, and letters to loved ones.

Hundreds of people read this and I heard from so many of them.

Some people sadly wished their loved ones had created such records before it was too late. Others added that they would give anything to read about the thoughts and emotions of the people they knew and loved before HD stole all that was recognizable.

Many families thought it was a great idea and they plan to do the same thing.

And then a couple of people told me that I was brave to head down this road, and that they admired my courage.

Now that last response had a huge impact on what I did next. See before, I had just been talking about being ready to start doing something. I wasn't in a place of action and could have easily found a million reasons to put this challenge off indefinitely.

But knowing that people exist who actually believe I can accomplish this dashed any hopes I had of bluffing my way out of it. I feel empowered and obligated to go through with the process, and I'll describe the experience here.

So, thanks to you, I have started making decisions about my future.

- I am considering a myriad of possibilities and contingencies. I have decided that I wouldn't enjoy choking to death, and how I'd much rather have a feeding tube. So there's one thing I'm sure of.

- But what if I was hospitalized for a non-H.D. related problem, like cancer, an injury, or a suicide attempt? My preferences would be different in this scenario. If there is a chance for my recovery, I want all the treatment I can get, and I want to be brought back if I crash. But if I'm on a life support machine with a poor prognosis, I want to be unplugged and not resuscitated.

- I have authorized my husband to carry out my wishes and have described how to determine that I am no longer able to make my own medical decisions.

- I have authorized the use of humane, comfortable restraints if I become violent. Under no circumstances will I be administered paralytic drugs. I also plan to compose a letter apologizing to my future medical care providers for my bad behavior and thanking them for helping me.

- I drafted a will and I'm ready to copy and paste it into the template which my state uses, I could not find this for free online, so a friend of mine who is an attorney agreed to score one for me.

It took several sittings and about a quart full of tears to get that far. But I was churning out pages at a steady pace.

Until today, when I started writing the first of three letters to each of my sons, I just had to stop for awhile. It became too personal and made everything seem real and impending. I began grieving the loss of participating "as me" in their futures.

It's too much to handle right now, which is why I came here for a break.

But I promise, when I regain composure, I will continue the process.

Because if some people believe I can do it, I want to prove them right.

# I have HD and I am mad

February 16, 2015

In the movement to raise awareness
for Huntington's Disease, sometimes it feels like there
aren't enough people outside of the bubble to help
spread the word. It's a rare delight to come across
a "normal person," like Melanie Nagy, who
has passion, the staying power and the attention span
to persevere. As for celebrities, James Franco, William
Shatner and John Cusack have pretty much spit in
my face.

It makes me angry, beating my head against a
brick wall, hoping to break through and let the light
shine on our community. But since anger is a
symptom of HD, I've tried to avoid using it as a tool
for raising awareness in order to make HD a more

"palatable" cause for the mainstream. But then again, maybe folks don't think HD is so bad because nobody is getting upset about it.

During the August HD Pie in the Face Challenge, James Franco had been given information about helping raise awareness for HD by his publicist's assistant (according to her), and it was his decision not to pursue it (again, according to her.) I reluctantly interpreted his lack of response as "Drop dead." His only involvement was when he (or a good impersonator) retweeted an HD Pie in the Face Challenge post on Twitter, which led many people to believe Franco actually started the challenge.

William Shatner cut and pasted something out of context from my blog and snidely replied that he'd pass. It was a frustrating miscommunication, because I wasn't asking for his money, but his help in raising awareness.

Then there was John Cusack, who used to be my favorite actor. I really blew that one. I twittered daily to ask for his non-monetary support. His fans told me to shut up and go away. It wasn't until my HD anger took over and I tweeted something not nice about him (I said that he shared certain features with the Grinch) that he responded directly to me, demanding to know what he ever did to me. I apologized profusely, explaining that I was frustrated, and simply trying to raise awareness for a horrible disease. But since this was not insulting to him, he did not respond. It turns out he only engages people who insult him. It is like a sport for him. But his fans responded, by the hundreds, mocking me, retweeting the exchange and telling me "How dare you..." I was in tears. And I figure John Cusack certainly watched the whole thing play out and did nothing to stop it. His "dogs" were attacking me. One Twitter angel contacted me and said that she googled HD and was sorry I had it and she would pray for me that night. I was angry, embarrassed and hurt, and to me she was the only one in the Twitterverse, and on that night, in the whole universe, who understood.

Perhaps later than I should have, I ended my attempts to attract celebrities to help raise awareness. Several high profile people who have HD dedicate some or all of their time to advocacy and I am grateful and appreciative for all they continually accomplish. But there isn't a living person with HD who is famous enough, I mean REALLY REALLY (Paul McCartney) FAMOUS enough, to inspire the world to lovingly look our way.

Attempts to draw "ordinary, healthy" people into raising HD awareness are almost as frustrating. One of my stepsons played T-ball and at the end of the year, he got a trophy. "Well," he said, "I finished that sport!" And never played baseball again because, in his mind, he had already done it.

There's that same disconnect with raising HD awareness: if someone has done one thing, they honestly believe they have done enough or done their part. They got the trophy.

But anyone who has watched the person they love be taken by HD knows that raising awareness shouldn't end with one Pie in the Face video or one shared HDSA page.

It should be something that people embrace and lobby for, work continually for, like what has happened with gay marriage and the use of medical marijuana. And those proponents were asking for legalization! The HD community is simply asking for acknowledgement.

Healthy neighbors and friends, who aren't caregivers, should advocate with us. People with emotional stability who perhaps won't draw the ire of John Cusack, but will instead use social media to share our stories and enlist further supporters. A few hundred healthy advocates working on a grassroots level could make a huge difference. If you're already out there somewhere, I want to know about you and thank you.

A new book is coming out by the author of "Still Alice", the story of a woman with alzheimer's disease which became a movie starring Julianne Moore. This next book is fictionalized tale of a family who has been impacted by Huntington's Disease. I think I read somewhere that the author has a background in neuroscience. Maybe she has found the Nicholas Sparks' formulaic equivalent of the neurodegenerative disease bestseller. I pray that she has. I hope that the book is a bestseller and that a movie is made, starring people (with Julianne Moore's acting chops) who will act out the experiences of an HD family for months while the movie is being filmed.

That's the closest anyone can get to having the experience without living it, and certainly the lives of those actors will be forever changed. And maybe they will tell the world.

But the book doesn't come out until April, and it will take a while for a movie to be made, if at all.

Meanwhile, the HD community is still largely in the shadows and nobody has won a trophy yet.

So do the amazing things that you know you can do. Then rest and repeat.

# I cannot live in a vacuum

March 5, 2015

The worsening of my condition is bearing down heavily on my littlest boy. He always seems to be around when I ask something a second time, sputter out odd sentences or get agitated. He matter-of-factly points out each new or blossoming symptom. He nags me if I perseverate, then I become irritable and that hurts his feelings.

He's come to realize that he's the only student in his fourth grade class who has this particular kind of mom waiting for him at home. Whereas in previous years he was popular and secure in school, he now feels isolated and misunderstood. He has headaches, stomach aches and sore throats each morning when it is time to go to school, but is healthy and energetic when he gets home.

The staff at his school is very supportive and he goes to him when his feelings overflow, which is happening more and more. He told the principal the that if there was a Zombie Apocalypse, he felt sure he would be the first person his class sacrificed to the zombies.

At the same time, he must also be mentally trying on my HD symptoms, wondering if, how and when he will deteriorate. It is all just too much for a boy of nine, or a boy of any age, to face without support.

So today, under the advice of my therapist, we took my son to an MD. We agree that he probably is physically healthy. Next we go to a therapist who has a track record of getting children to open up by circumnavigating the issues while engaging in safe discussions.

A lot of other things could be going on instead or as well. It's time to get a new prescription for his glasses and he hasn't been wearing them, so he could be actually having headaches. He has difficulty paying attention in class and says there is too much noise for him to concentrate, so there could be some attention deficit going on. At home he demands constant attention and I remember that my two older boys became clingy at around this age. Maybe he instinctively knows that puberty is on the way and this is our last chance for mom and little boy interactions. I ought to cherish each one. I want to.

Trouble is, I don't interact well or often. I rarely initiate conversation, and can't keep up with the flow of changing topics. A lot of times I will just stay home, just as much to keep my family from having to see me taking the down escalator as to experience the satisfaction that I only feel when I am home.

Last weekend, I stayed home on Saturday, but Sunday, I took a 40 minute ride with my husband and son to the ocean. I sat in the car while they explored a Civil War fort and sat in the car again while they checked out an enormous barge being guided through a strip of deep water by tugboats. I hope they knew that my being there at all was an act of love.

When they returned, I enjoyed hearing about their adventures. But then we went into a restaurant, which I haven't done in some time. I felt depersonalized, like I was standing behind this ever changing version of myself and watching her trying to operate outside the vacuum. Outside of the security of the familiar places, home and routine. My therapist said that I could have been depersonalizing to protect myself from something. And this is it:

For the first time, I knew other people could tell that there was definitely something wrong with me. And I couldn't handle being "present" for that.

But in the weeks to come, I must pull myself out of my comfortable, safe vacuum to create and activate a support system for my son.

He'll need a whole lot of support to keep his life on track as he watches mine slowly fade away.

# CRISIS TIME

March 18, 2015

I have been doing horribly inappropriate things. I can't make myself not do them, but after I've acted inappropriately, I can see where I acted wrong. But then I can't take back the actions and the damage is done forever. No one understands how it is a symptom of HD, even if I explain the whole caudate nucleus thing to them. They think it is my personality.

I do not want to be this person. I don't think it is who I am or who I want to be. I do not want to put my husband and children through this.

I have called all three numbers for the therapist and the psychiatrist and I am waiting  by the phone. My therapist called and reminded me that I am a good person, and if I wasn't I wouldn't be bothered by what I was doing. She says the people who know me know its HD. But what about the rest of town? Does my life before me contain a series of increasingly inappropriately events? I believe that is the prognosis. But faced with it, I don't want any part of it.

Cannot continue to live this way, and would prefer being a zombie to becoming the monster I'm becoming.

You would think that if I can recognize the social disruption and inappropriateness of my actions after the fact, I would learn, the next time something came around, to not make the same mistake again.

But I go there again and again. Faced with the impulse, I cannot stop myself.

Last night a man down the street walked into his neighbor's house with a machete and hacked a woman's three sons to bits. This scene has been playing over and over in my mind today, and I feel so badly for the family but so grateful my children are safe.

Still, the moment I act, concerning this, it is inappropriate and hurtful to other people.

I am instantly filled with shame and remorse.

I cannot perform the work that I have been assigned  because I don't trust the way I will behave when I deal with the folks I am helping out. What unexpected hell might I come up with to ruin their day? All I know is that a change of meds can only help.

I don't know what awful thing I'll allow myself to do tomorrow, and it is frightening. I am sorry to the people whose lives I've negatively impacted.

I just want some antipsychotic that will erase the urge to act out, even if it erases who I am.

It will be worth it, and it might just be the only way I'll be able to continue my life. Because I can't continue living on this path. I am not strong. I am not brave. I have no answers for anything. I am weak and scared and I need help.

I have a bottle of Risperdal that I had decided not to use, and in absence of any medical advice, I have taken one, and I hope it changes the way I behave. If it doesn't  I need to know what other options I have to protect people from me.

# Waking up to a blue sky

March 19, 2015

Emotionally hungover.

Usually when my friends contact me because they are alarmed by something I have written here, I feel badly for getting them all worked up and worried. A lot of what I write is contemplative or an attempt to transcribe a feeling and not a cry for help.

That wasn't the case last night and today. I have subsisted on offerings of love and reassurance from my friends. They, and other HD families, understand.

But I don't think that I really "got" it until today.

I'm trying to suppress out of control behaviors, knowing that they have hurt others. Someone described them to me as "mini-aggressions." I told that person I wanted to stop the mini aggressions forever and learned that what I wanted was as likely as wanting the sky to be pink and waking up to a pink sky.

HD is upon me now. So much of my brain has been damaged and the damage will only progress and my symptoms will only get worse.

My reassuring fantasies about possibly having a kinder, gentler, HD have been wiped away like so many hot, salty tears.

It boils down to two questions.

1. How long can what is left of my brain compensate for the part that is damaged?

2. Or have I passed that point already?

# What I did while you were at church

March 22, 2015

New medicine, perhaps, makes this morning consecutive moments of realization.

Like a skipping record, I go back to the point where the barbed truth abrades me. I am sitting on my own shoulder, witnessing my brain tearing itself apart. The curtain of my life, as I ever knew it, is closing fast, and I don't have long to say what needs to be said, to get all of the thoughts out that I want to convey in this lifetime.

My claws hold me in place, so I can stay to say enough times, adequately enough and so they won't forget, to the people I love, that I love them so much.

And now I realize that's what it was all about and I am sorry for having misplaced my attention and my affection.

There is the possibility that the curtain has already closed, and what I think are my last words as my old self are instead the first from the new, demented me. That part of me has maybe taken over and the truth just hasn't caught up with me yet.

I look back at my life as no one else who knows me sees it, as snapshots of nights filled with drunken laughter, broken hearts, aimless living,

The faces of people I lived with and loved run across the screen I am watching and I am comforted by remembering the shared epiphanies, the bonds of friendship that distance doesn't break. So many people twho I may never see or talk to again, but still love so dearly.

Now, two people are left and I want to fill them up with everything I never said but know that they would explode if I did that.

The time for doing that is passing by me now, if I haven't missed it already.

When it becomes too late, I'll be misunderstood. I will communicate through a series of emotional explosions until the people that are left can't bear to see it anymore, or are simply torn apart and tired.

At that point, I wonder if I'll have enough self left to be disappointed with myself, or will my consciousness just be a primal world, suitable for what is left of my brain.

I start to slip into thinking that none of it matters. That it is all misfiring synapses and sleep deprivation.

I shove it all into a corner of my mind and go on with my day.

# Dear receptionist,

March 25, 2015

I have Huntington's Disease.

I look like everyone else except the truth is that proteins are killing off parts of my brain.

In my case, I have difficulty processing spoken words and finding the right words in a timely manner.

This afternoon I went to check in at my doctor's family practice and the you, the receptionist, caught me off guard with an insurance question that I couldn't process. I heard it when you said that medicare was always right. The only response I could think of or that I could get to come out of my mouth was, "The computer is wrong."

So I kept saying that and you thought I was mad at you and you got flustered and defensive. Then I started to panic and breathe really hard. I bet I scared you and if I did, I am sorry. I was scared, too. I didn't know how I was going to see the doctor if this went on forever.

I was not mad at you, but I could still only verbalize that one sentence, "The computer is wrong."

I got out my phone so my husband could communicate with you on my behalf. But when you saw me with the phone you quickly called the office manager to come from the other building.

The office manager came out and began explaining to me about the insurance but she thought I was mad at everyone, too. I guess I looked mad, but I felt scared and alone.

So I mentally checked out and gave her the phone.

When it was my turn to see the doctor, I went back to the nurse's station and cried for a long time because I knew this is just the beginning of my decline and already it is so hard to cope with people's reactions to my behavior.

I am writing this so maybe you can understand that I have a brain disease that affects my oral communication as well as my level of frustration. I have worked in customer service and know how mean people can be. It hurts to know that you and the office manager think I was being mean or aloof.

At some point I will not be able to see the doctor without help but I am not there yet. My regular doctor is wasn't there, otherwise I'm sure she would've let you know about my situation and that I am harmless.

I wish more people understood HD and could step up for me. I would sure have appreciated it yesterday.

I am not alone in this community and maybe I am writing this because I want to make it easier for the next person who has HD and comes to your window to check in.

Since I can still write, I might just have to write a note to keep in my pocket to give people when misunderstood.

Because it is just going to get worse, I know. And then people won't even talk to me because they know something is wrong with me, but they don't want to go near it.

But I don't think I will be sadder when that happens than I was today. Very truly yours.

# Untitled

So I haven't written in a while because I am getting worse in about every way I can.

But before I complain about it, I must acknowledge that I am lucky that my progression is slower than other people and that HD is hitting me later in life than it could.

I pray for everyone else who is suffering worse than I am. The people who got tested today. The people who got their results today. The people who lost their loved ones today.

Everything is sort of going at the same time, some things gradually, like swallowing and some things not, like Impulse control. The guy at Jiffy Lube didn't believe I wasn't drunk.

It feels like I'm short circuiting. It is harder to find the words when I am writing. I am starting to spell words funny. Like I spelled the word "damn" as "damb" which I kind of like better, after the shock wore off.

I feel a big change coming on and I can't describe it. I've lost the ability.

I do know that I feel really really tired. And I have for days. Just tired to the bone.

I hope I get better and can write again. Not being able to write is my greatest fear.

# A hole in the community fabric

April 21, 2015

For the past 5 years, Craven Community College in New Bern, NC has gathered practically the whole town at the Convention Center, fed us a really good lunch, and then bestowed three Community Fabric Awards to community, business and academic leaders who have done really great things for our town.

I always look forward to going. I love New Bern and this is a happy event where we celebrate our sense of community. Lots of events take place at the Convention Center, and most people go to all of them, so many faces are familiar by now. I like being within smiling distance of lots of acquaintances and show the goodwill without trying to have a conversation, because I never know how my words will come out.

But when things were winding down, I was a little disappointed that I hadn't had the chance to connect with anyone not sitting at my table. Just because I dread speaking doesn't mean I don't want to connect.

And that's one of the reasons I'm so glad you came by when you did.

The program had just ended when you came up to me, smiling, and said, "Sarah, I just came by to say 'Hi!'" And then you were gone.

You shot off like a cork from a bottle of champagne before I could see which way you went, and when I asked my husband which way you went, he said he hadn't seen you at all!

I was sitting all the way in the front, and we were already forming ant lines to march to our cars.

You were very kind to go out of your way to connect with me.

But I don't remember your name or recognize your face.

Even though I've probably met you and talked with you a dozen times. By the way you smiled at me, I could tell that you know I have HD, and that maybe you even read this blog. I hope you read this.

I don't know who you are but you still made my day special. I have the feeling you understand.

Instead of conceding that dead parts of my brain now serve as a colander for certain memories, I have made a happier choice: I got a surprise visit from a secret friend.

That way I don't cry.

# One of these days the cure is gonna come

April 27, 2015

One of these days the cure is gonna come.

We'll be following every move. Or it will take us by surprise. At first we won't let our hopes afloat because they've been dashed many times by waves of disappointment.

But the cure is gonna come.

Right now, people we will never know are working as if *their* lives depended on it, racing to cure us.

Our babies and us.

They don't sleep much and they know more about HD than we ever want to know. And they are out there now, all over the world, helping us.

Our babies and us.

When the cure comes, we rejoice, cry tears of joy for our children and bitter tears for those for whom the cure was too late.

There are screams the neighbors can hear, and an internet celebration that will never, ever end.

We line up to be saved, and we save all the children first. The ones who suffer now and then the ones at risk.

Then it is our turn. We smile and take a leap of faith through the treatment and into...

## What it's like to lose myself

May 11, 2015

I have a strong sense of detachment from the woman who usually interacts with my family.

That person is so unfamiliar now. Sometimes I just let out a wail, then pull myself together.

I have to push against that person so she will care, do, act, and move. But then she forgets, drops, stumbles and writhes.

She has started pushing back harder and is becoming less familiar. She has done some things I never would have done and left me feeling ashamed because who would believe that she did them instead of me?

She is reeling in more and more of my day. I have to dedicate extra time for her to sleep, so she will not harm people. Now I nap and go to bed early because me and my family are safe from her when I'm asleep.

Only when I write do I get any distance from her when I'm awake. It's like hiding out in a tree house with a laptop.

When I write I feel more situated in Sarah. My brain is doing a familiar thing. I can turn her off that way sometimes.

But so many times she has slithered through and insinuated herself anyway, right here on this screen. You've seen it.

Just now I set out to explain my feelings and alienation using the metaphor of another person.

But she argues that *she* is the one who wanted me to tell you about her.

# Perfecting the art of forgetting

May 17, 2015

While a lot of symptoms are starting to emerge, the one that is interfering with "Life as I Knew It" the most is memory loss.

### The list of things forgotten.

First, I stopped being able to remember things people just said to me, even if they'd said those things multiple times. Then I stopped being able to remember names of my neighbors and coworkers. Now I forget entire conversations, including all the information the other person has shared and my observations and responses to hearing that information. Sometimes when I respond to something someone has told me, I will remember having responded that way before and I'll say, "Oops, we've had this conversation before." These days, with my family, I will forget a decision we just made. I'll reintroduce people. I'll say things over and over. I try to keep track of life by using context clues, checking, reconfirming, reviewing, writing it down (when possible), or, when my husband is around, saying, "Randy, I need to remember this thing."

**Sounding the buzzer.**

As soon as I remember what I want to say, I interrupt the conversation in progress and change the topic, saying, "Sorry but I have to get this out because I just remembered it." A lot of times before I get to the end of this apology/explanation, I can only remember part of the sentence I was going to say, or just the topic.

**Twenty questions about topics.**

Often I will only remember the topic of a thing that I wanted to discuss with someone. So I say, for example, "I can't remember, but it has to do with medicine," or, more recently, "Medicine." Whomever I'm talking with suggests ideas related to medicine. They ask, "Are you out of medicine?" I say no. They ask, "Do you need to take your medicine?" I say no. This continues until they come across what I wanted to say or I just say, "Nevermind." What happens next varies. A few minutes later, I might sound the buzzer with the answer: "I spilled my medicine on the floor." But it might take seeing the pills on the floor to bring the memory back. And sometimes I never remember what the hell I wanted to say.

**Ask for a redo.** When all else fails, I'll just come straight out and ask the person, "I know you've told me many times before, but could you please tell me (an important fact that was a pivotal moment in that person's life.)" I know that I do several redos about the same things every day. Usually I get that "ahhhhh" feeling as people retell me, but sometimes they say, "Hey we've discussed this several times today," but I had no idea. In fact, if I didn't trust them more than my memory, I'd say they were lying.

**Blame the brain.** In an effort to delineate the boundaries of my personality from the memory damage caused by HD, I have these conversations: "I know it must be very frustrating for you to have to say things again and again. If I had the choice, it wouldn't be that way." My littlest boy is almost ten, and when I asked him if my lack of memory was annoying, he admitted that it was. I told him how sorry I was and made sure he knew that my memory "has a mind of its own" and I, his mother, really wish things could be different. That's a bitter kind of consolation, but I want to acknowledge other people's feelings while I still have that ability.

**Cut myself some slack.** My dad had a stroke and during the 10 years before he died, he operated on a three minute memory loop. His humor was left intact. But my mom, who has an angry HD, did not think any of dad's jokes were funny. In fact, his jokes enraged her. She gave him hell, he gave her sheepish looks, and in a minute or so looked at her and repeated the joke. He had reset and they played the whole thing out again and again. When I'd visit my dad, he'd make the same joke about himself, "I have CRS: Can't Remember Shit!" with an exaggerated grin of pride. So now I have my own form of CRS, and it's up to me to deal with it. I could throw my hands up in despair. Sometimes I do.

Or I could embrace my CRS for what it is and continue to practice perfecting the art of forgetting.

# Just because

May 28, 2015

Just because I pour my heart out doesn't make me any different from you.

Just because I write about it doesn't mean I get rid of it.

Just because I cry a lot doesn't make me weak.

Just because my words run together doesn't mean that my thoughts aren't clear.

Just because I don't remember you doesn't mean I am gullible.

Just because you share my blood doesn't mean I'll ever let you attack me again.

Just because you "knew me when" doesn't mean you know me now.

Just because I can't answer your question doesn't mean that I've failed.

Just because I agree with you doesn't mean I'm in your pocket.

Just because I forget something doesn't mean I never knew it.

Just because my brain cells are dying doesn't mean I can be brainwashed.

Just because I like you doesn't mean I only like who you like.

Just because I wake up in a nightmare doesn't mean I can't love all the people in it.

# I went on a "real world" safari and lived to tell about it

June 1, 2015

I spend a lot of time at home.

Days slide together into weeklong patches of time and that is how I live.

In a vaguely organized blur.

It's hard to assess my abilities and disabilities when I'm in my element because I have a poor memory of fleeting variations in my routine.

This past weekend's Paddle for HD to benefit HD Reach was a good chance to test my abilities in an unfamiliar setting.

Between 30 and 40 kayakers showed up. Many were dear friends, old and new. But people also came who did not know me. I wasn't wearing a sign or T-Shirt that indicated I have Huntington's disease, and I blended into the scenery for the most part.

In addition to my husband, all three of my sons were there. We are not all together frequently, so this added to my joy. The oldest spent the whole event sort of keeping me in check. For instance, before people got there, I started inexplicably running from one place to another to get things done. Like Edith Bunker.

"Mom, stop running! You're going to fall down!" my oldest said. And he was right. There was no reason to run around like crazy. It took him saying this a few times for it to register, but I slowed things down and even went to sit down at the registration table.

I was afraid that, when my friends arrived, I'd feel torn and confused and would ignore my duties in an attempt to make them feel welcomed. But they arrived with satisfied smiles and a predetermined mission: to get in kayaks and hit the water. So I guess I passed the test of our first encounter, even though it was because their arrival belied my expectations.

My oldest son stayed right with me during the whole event. He didn't leave my side unless I asked him to take some photographs or help carry a kayak. He helped me when I got confused counting raffle tickets. He helped me write the names and numbers on the raffle tickets of late-comers. And, according to my husband, my oldest did not get into a kayak until much later in the day, when I did. He anticipated my every need and I felt supported but not coddled. I'll admit that I could not have functioned at the capacity I did without his help.

The only time I got frazzled was during the raffle. Earlier, I delegated it to someone else, but then forgot I had delegated it and kept participating in the pulling of raffle tickets and the distribution of prizes. I quickly became confused with the process and then panicked. It wasn't going the way I'd planned. In fact, I'd forgotten to make a plan for the drawing.

Then I realized that the only person who was confused was me. So I consciously stepped away and let it happen without me.

And, when I stepped away and let things happen differently, the world continued.

And things got better. Even though I stumbled, shuffled and swayed a bit, my friends didn't seem to notice. They were all so happy to be together for such a great occasion on a perfect day.

There were times when I stammered or couldn't find the words I wanted, and sometimes it sounded like I was talking with my mouth full of marbles. But I was surrounded by people who know me and care about me and about each other.

It was not all about me.

It was about high school and college friends being together. It was about old friends meeting new friends. It was about avid kayakers learning about HD. It was about helping HD Reach, an organization that helps so many people in NC.

I was symptomatic in the real world, but I made it.

Instead of wondering if or how my symptoms were being perceived, I focused on the event and enjoyed each moment

I love all those people who came. They accepted and supported me.

Same time next year?

# My right foot

June 6, 2015

My left foot stands firmly in the present while the right one dangles precariously over the entrance to my dark impending descent into madness.

I'm buying groceries and notice how hard it is becoming. I imagine the inevitability of doing or saying something that will make me unwelcome here.

While I talk to the barber about my son's haircut, I preoccupy myself by wondering if the barber can tell that I'm preoccupied.

As I walk with my family in our neighborhood, a low branch skewers my head. My riddled, pissed off brain shoos away the branch and I'm feeling more and more like Edgar Allen Poe may have felt without the opium.

I sit for hours, as other people live, and I just wait for it …

An ending to the way I feel. Some sort of closure.

But that's not very likely. HD doesn't present respite wrapped in bows. It is more akin to a box of snakes, serving up fear and trouble.

Everything I have done today has been in an effort to ignore my right foot.

There isn't enough sleep. Enough family. Enough food. Enough Avatar by James Cameron… No means of escape.

Just as I am about to collapse, the right leg comes over and wraps around my left one like a bull whip and shores up my balance.

I just sit down, glassy eyed, and let my legs unravel.

# The extra album track

I've been thinking a lot lately, as spring melts into summer, about changes I want to make in my life. I've realized that more of my day-to-day dissatisfactions are caused by my reaction to having Huntington's disease than HD itself.

Some caregivers say that their loved ones with HD faced it bravely from the start, showed strength through every phase of the journey, were gracious and tried to hold on to a healthy quality of life.

Not me.

I found out I had HD in 2010 and for a solid year I was in a deep, fearful depression. I was useless to my family, a burden, even. I couldn't see beyond my own problems to those of my family and I complained about everything. I became sedentary.

Eventually, after finding a therapist who is ass-kicking good (and I know you are reading this and you are AWESOME!), I pulled out of the depression, but remained sedentary and continued to medicate myself (or try to kill myself) with food.

Especially ice cream. I ballooned and have stayed inflated and sedentary during the intervening years. I went through a bad emotional patch around Easter, and upped my ice cream intake. My cocoon grew.

Now I am starting to show a lot more HD symptoms but the main visible damage has been self-inflicted.

Every single person in my life has told me that there is only one thing known to slow progression of HD and that is exercise. My best friends have offered to be exercise buddies and I have ignored them. My husband tried kindly to encourage me but I always had an excuse or if I didn't, I would play the HD card. I resisted until, finally, I outgrew my fat clothes and noticed that I had to turn sideways to walk between tables at a restaurant. I was fed up.

It's hard to describe the moment of change, except to say that my therapist acted as a psychological chiropractor of sorts, and one day she said something that made me snap into a mode of action, where I have been ever since.

For the better part of the last three weeks, my husband has walked at my pace, as much or as little as I wanted, through our beautiful neighborhood with its tree-lined streets.

Today, after our walk, I got the first endorphin rush I've had in years. It brought back the sense memories of living in a healthy body. One that could run 5 miles and do 90 minutes of Bikram yoga in the front row of a hot room.

So I pulled out a yoga mat and turned on You Tube.

My wonderful sister-in-law, who I love and who knows how to be healthy, suggested that I freeze mango chunks and eat them instead of ice cream. The coldness on my palate is just as addictive as the ice cream. Last week I consumed one large family-sized container of ice cream a day for three days. Finally, I asked myself as I threw away an empty container, "How do you think this is going to end?"

I didn't like the answer and the next day I went to the store and bought a lot of mangoes. Every time I want to eat ice cream, I have a little frozen mango. It works.

All of this is to admit that I still have quite a bit of life left to enjoy.

And I plan to.

# … and who doesn't love a parade?

June 18, 2015

I am not going to be afraid anymore because I am sick of it. And I am sick of worrying about being sick.

Today I glanced at impending doom and chose to look away instead of letting it mesmerize me. I slammed the door on something sinister, something that wanted to snatch away everything that I have.

And it has made me so tired.

I'm tired of being terrified of my perseverations, and from now on, I am going to challenge them. Fear will no longer be my default emotion. I'll try to harvest some energy from bravery, if it comes close enough for me to grab it.

I know I'll never escape HD.  But I have something good starting up and I am putting together some good days. Happy days. Days that don't require white knuckles and contingency plans. I am nobody's burden. Not even my own. Because I have had enough of that.

I remind myself that it's not my fault that I have Huntington's disease. I reassure myself that I have taken measures to treat the symptoms, even if, today, it was just in the nick of time.

Time.  Today I see it not as a force of destruction, but as a friend, a gift.

A  parade that should be celebrated as it passes.

# When the psychiatrist who totally "gets" you moves on

June 23, 2015

It was an email I didn't expect, and it stated that my psychiatrist was no longer going to see patients and that I will need to obtain (with assistance) a different psychiatrist.

Mine isn't just any psychiatrist. She is regarded as one of, if not the, finest psychiatrists specializing in HD in the country. But it is not her reputation that makes this separation sad.

It is the fact that she lived up to it – and more- in her interactions with me.

And I don't know what I'm going to do now.

She was sharp enough, years ago, to tell me that the symptoms I was reporting had nothing to do with HD. I had Post Traumatic Stress Disorder. Oddly, it was a relief to hear that, because it was something non-genetic that could be fixed. It could be battled with success, unlike the progression of HD.

So off I went, with my hometown, kickass therapist and slayed some dragons. Life became much easier.

When the HD symptoms did start to show up, my psychiatrist exhibited a nearly supernatural insight into the disease that she tapped into time and again as she explained HD to my husband and me. She described what was happening in my brain and how that was impacting my short term memory, executive functioning, emotional regulation, perseveration, impulse control, and speech. These are some of the symptoms that I exhibit. So often in my blog I focus on a moment, or a feeling, but I've never really laid the whole picture out. Now seems like as good a time as any for that.

My psychiatrist also trained my husband and me to work together in more ways than I can enumerate. For example, I can use his brain to store certain information. He has learned several cues, techniques, red flags, and coping strategies. He can try to redirect me when I perseverate and make sure I take my evening meds on time.

She empowered us, she totally got us, and now she is moving on.

I know that she will stay true to form and facilitate a smooth transition. And the most comforting fact is that she will not be completely out of my life.

But I know in future crises, when I am just about to lose my grip,hers will be the voice and words I'll pretend to hear, no matter who is on the other end of the phone or in the emergency room.

And that's what's going to save me.

# The red water bottle

June 27, 2015

I woke up at 6, had breakfast, drove down to the all night pharmacy to get the "important" medicine I would have run out of otherwise. Came home and had coffee and an introspective conversation. I went for a walk with my family, as has become our habit, and when we get back...

Let me back up a minute and tell you that I constantly drink water from a red water bottle with a straw tube and a plastic mouthpiece. I have used it for a couple of years. We have several other water bottles but this is the one I like and if I use another one or cannot find the red water bottle I am not happy.

Well, typically when we return from a walk, I will stay on the front porch with the poodle while someone will go in for water and come out with my red bottle filled. We'll sit on the porch and sip until we've cooled down enough to go inside. Any deviation from this routine makes me anxious.

But yesterday. when we returned from a long drive, I had left the red bottle in the car. I knew it was in the car, but I thought about not knowing *exactly* where the bottle was during the whole walk and by the time we got home from the walk, I was already feeling agitated about the bottle. I asked my son to run in and use the automatic key to unlock the car from inside the house so I could get it. It took a really, really long time for this to happen, and by then, I was irritable. When I could not find the bottle in the car, my heart started beating really fast and I felt sick. I asked my husband to look in the car.

He didn't find it either and assured me that it would turn up, then set about to complete his many tasks.

I filled another bottle and drank until I was no longer thirsty. But I am mad at the bottle for not being my red bottle. All the others are hard to drink from or leak or don't feel right in my hand and some of them don't have straws so I have to throw my head back to drink.

I am sitting in the living room and the OTHER BOTTLE is sitting on the dining room table, with water in it, but banished from my inner circle.

Not having my red cup has made other things that have happened seem painful. I couldn't find the stamps and I nearly cried. We might be out of address labels and I feel helpless. I am waiting for a phone call and an email and I am covered in congealed sweat and I feel like a prisoner. I am getting really depressed. The "Uh oh" kind of depression that puts a stop to the flow of the day. I don't cry because tears would understate the anguish that I feel.

And it's all because I can't find my red bottle. I know if it suddenly appeared, I would relax, my emotions would regulate and I would drink a lot of water. But there is no guarantee that it will turn up and I can't get past that.

It's just not happening the way it's supposed to.

# Tips for traveling with HD

July 27, 2015

I wish I could leave HD behind when I travel but I can't. That's why, more and more, I tend to avoid traveling. But this year I've been traveling quite a bit, maybe because each experience informs me that my days of independent travel are numbered.

Trial and error this summer helped me compile this list of ideas to make traveling with HD easier. Many tips may seem obvious, but I now have to consciously consider things that used to be automatic or rote.

**1. Inventory meds.** A week before my trip, I compare the level of pills in each bottle to the pill dispenser I will take on the the trip. If it looks like I am going to run short, I call the pharmacy or doctor right then to get refills.

**2. Pack early and often.** Functionally, I can't pack all at once, but I make a list of what I need in my suitcase and put it by the bag several days before the trip. As I pack the items, I cross them off the list. In real life, I don't use drawers. Instead I have my clothes sitting out where I can see them, so I can remember what I have. I go through my clothes, remove what I will take, wash clothes in the laundry bin that are coming on the trip and then display everything on a chair in my bedroom where I can look at it and see that I have it there, ready. (If you haven't traveled in a few years, be aware that the US has begun to make you check bags that are a little larger than backpacks and charge you at least $25 per bag, so pack small.)

**3. Strive for comfort.** I've decided I'm only going to wear clothes that are easy to travel and move around in because I have enough to worry about without trying to pull off fashion statements. I have a couple pairs of Skecher "Go Walk" shoes that I can walk in without tripping too much, so I'll wear and bring them, along with athletic shoes for anything strenuous. Traveling in slip-on shoes also provides a moment of relief when shoes must come off in airport security.

**4. Give everyone emergency numbers.** I have all of my emergency numbers, like my psychiatrist, therapist, and pharmacist, programmed into my phone, but I think I will email them to my traveling companion or host so if I have a problem I can't handle, they will know who to call in what order.

**5. Be a card carrier.** Along the same lines, if I become tongue-tied, I have learned that I need something that I can shove into an impatient airport employee's face before it explodes. WeHaveAFace.org has a simple ID card you can download. It is dark print on a white background and is easy to read. I am going to laminate mine.

**6. Stay hydrated despite airport security.** Just before going through security, I empty my beloved water bottle and let it run through the x-ray machine. As soon as I retrieve it, I go to the nearest water fountain and fill it up!

**7. Create a kit.** I remove everything from my purse and set it aside. I pack only my wallet with my ID right on top, medication, phone and charger, other device and charger, a print-out of my itinerary so I can check and re-check, boarding passes, snacks from home and my water bottle.

**8. Ask for extra assistance x 2.** Number 1) I ask the people who drop me off at the airport to help me check in. All it takes is one unexpected question from the airport staff and my brain goes into panic mode and my mouth shuts down. Number 2) After a harrowing experience of "swimming upstream" 10 rows during boarding, I now ask for special assistance at the gate when I check in. This just gives me piece of mind to have extra time to find my seat without worrying about holding up the other passengers.

**9. Minimize connections.** Direct is best, but If I have connections, I ask at the arrival gate how to get to my destination gate and head straight there. If you have mobility issues, you can ask airport personnel to summon a cart to take your next gate. They are pretty fast.

**10. H.A.L.T.** Avoid being **H**ungry, **A**ngry, **L**onely, or **T**ired. I have access to food and water, my medications, and my HD ID card. Sometimes, angry just happens and I might have to call one of my friends to help me calm down. I will get plenty of rest the night before and use flying time as relaxation time.

# "There ARE no apologies, Mom."

August 22, 1015

I never write about my mother for a couple of reasons. The first is that she still lives. The second is "if you can't say anything nice, don't say anything at all."

For years in my childhood I experienced a frightful relationship with my mother, one that turned contentious as I grew older. Now that I know that there's a good chance all of her behaviors stemmed from the personality changes caused by HD, I still find myself unable to forgive. Even though she is now docile and kind. I think of the damage done as the nail holes left behind after a picture is removed from a wall.

When I was younger, I have to say that the vantage point I observed my mother from was too close. I was too close to her and too easily influenced by her to consider, for a moment, that she had HD. My reasoning?

My mother was already a bitch.

She was mean and hateful since I was about 8 or so. Mama would insult my friends and hang up on them, yell at me, my brother and my dad. She didn't use 90% of the businesses in town because they had done something to piss her off.

She wasn't on speaking terms with any of the neighbors. In fact one of them planted a tree right in the middle of the pathway that connected the two houses.

Mama tried to run off every boyfriend and husband that I brought into the house. She refused to acknowledge the existence of my third son, until he was able to speak to her and she had no choice.

Those symptoms could not be Huntington's related, I rationalized, because they appeared too early. And what kind of world would make someone so mean and then give them HD? It did not seem congruent and therefore I denied HD as a possibility in her life.

Later I learned that personality changes can occur long before chorea begins, but by then she had done a whole lot of damage to so many people.

People told me that, once, she was actually a nice, warm person, who would, for example,  drive an hour to meet you at a train station and give you a homemade pineapple upside down cake.

I never knew that woman.

My brother is her devoted caregiver and God bless him. I stay in touch, but concentrate on my own family and my own children, Unlike my mom, I have never threatened to strangle my children or to throw them out of a moving car. I've spent more energy that it would take most people to be kind to my kids, both because I want to and because I can feel my fuse getting shorter.

Nonetheless, HD is spilling out at them in ways I don't like. Last night, for instance, I cursed angrily at my youngest son for moving a pillow. I was instantly remorseful and told him I was sorry. This was not the first time I had blown a fuse at him in the evening before my meds kicked in. His response jolted me. "There ARE no apologies, Mom," he said and I realized he was right.

My mother never apologized to me for anything she did. Maybe it is not within her capacity. It's a lot harder to forgive someone when they don't apologize. I have lost many relatives to HD who were loving and kind, despite occasional angry outbursts. I think of them instead of my mother when I try to relate to other people's anguish over losing a loved one to HD and the purity of their love for that person.

And I remind myself every day that I am not my mother and my path may be very different. But it's hard at times like these, when I watch myself snip away little bits of my son's own self-worth and much less, his love for me.

And he is right.

There really are no apologies.

# What my employers don't know

September 3, 2015

Every time I start to write this blog, I get work to do and have to stop. But that's good news. I got a work from home job that is keeping me busy. Due to confidentiality agreements, the most I can say is that I got a part-time freelance writing job. The people I work for are wonderful, intelligent and friendly. And I enjoy the work itself.

Unless my employers googled me, they don't know I have HD. (If they have, hello!) They don't know that I have been through Vocational Rehabilitation. They don't know that I have an amazing Easter Seals Job Coach, Erica, who calls me regularly and comes to visit me. They don't know that I am being supported by a kick-ass therapist and that I am on great meds. They don't know that my brain seems to have rewired itself so that now I have regained some abilities I thought I'd lost. They have heard my slurred and halting speech but don't know the cause.

I am experiencing the joy of being HD free in one aspect of my life and it is rejuvenating my spirit.

But how long can this last? A large part of being new at a job is forgetting things and making mistakes. The same can be said of HD. If they exist together on the learning curve, what is going to happen when my ride on this curve ends? Will I be able to retain the skills that other employees retain (with my support system), or will it become obvious that something is wrong with me?

I don't know that answer, but I am doing everything I can, using every resource I can think of, especially my husband's brain, to enhance the

possibility of success.

# Steady-as-she-goes

September 13, 2015

I have wanted to write for so long, but I still haven't gotten the hang of doing more than my job, on the computer, at least.

So what I write today goes towards the creation of a counterweight so there can be a new balance struck.

I've been working a lot, but in addition to that, some real life things are happening that approximate a normal life. I am going on semi-regular bicycle rides around the neighborhood with my husband. Bicycle riding now has the thrill of motorcycle riding, without the additional cost. When I make a turn, share traffic with cars, and cross intersections, there is an exhilaration that is about 75% fear and 25% "I can do this."

I also have a wonderful neighbor and friend who knows I used to love gardening, but that this love has been blunted by HD, She is dauntless in facing me and my disease. She shows up with carloads of offshoots from her garden, a bandana, and a shovel. How can I not muster enthusiasm when it takes human form and knocks on my door? So suddenly, there are new inhabitants in the yard to check on and water. My goal is to someday have no yard for my husband to have to mow. I have lots of time to make that happen.

When another wonderful neighbor moved away, (I live in a great neighborhood where everyone is friends) she gave me some paint. I decided to tackle the project of painting the downstairs bathroom, no matter what color the paint was. The bathroom is now kermit-the-frog green and after three months, I'm not finished yet, but that's OK. I've got lots of time.

Despite progress in other areas, I find that unless my mind is transfixed on something, intrusive and unpleasant thoughts creep in. At night, I am particularly vulnerable, so I'm being careful about taking my medicine on time. Last night I got stuck on being stuck on things, and wound up on Craigslist, which is like falling into a briar patch of things to perseverate about.

Before too long, I had a boat picked out, A 42-foot 1978 trawler, which is insanely out of the ballpark of our budget and our mutually agreed on financial plans. My husband reminded me of this several times, and I responded, "I know, but I still can't stop thinking about it." It is like an itch I can never come close to reaching. A yearning I can't come close to describing. Last month it was a pair of shoes I didn't need and this month it is a boat I'm not buying.

Tomorrow will come work, which keeps my mind focused on something that it should be doing and I brings with it the hope that things will continue going as well as they are now.

For as long as possible ...

# Kicking and screaming

September 23, 2015

Work has sucked me into it as much as social media ever has. I feel like I have abandoned my Facebook friends by not being there in the event that they needed support. I went to my son's open house yesterday and everyone said, "I haven't seen you in forever." So I guess I feel like a productive dropout. Now my life is unbalanced in the other direction, with a truckload of work tipping the scales. With HD, it is not like I can just do one thing and not the other. I have to do something so much I wear a hole in the ground around myself. I have tunnel vision and I am not letting go of my work.

Far away are my friends, who say they are proud of me, who I hope will understand that I am not intentionally blowing them off. Instead I have a frenzied need to perform all of the work that there is to work. To sell all of my words.

To be kicking and screaming the day that I can't work because that will be my nadir.

There are discomforts to be ignored right now, like lack of sleep, and relentless deadlines and just having a tired brain that seems to take too long. Then there are harder things to overlook, like calling my son's art teacher Ms. Fiorina when she is not a GOP candidate. Like the thickness in my tongue when I speak.

But this morning when I got out of bed, the thing happened which I could not ignore: I could not walk a straight line. I staggered and did the dance all the way down the stairs and hit walls and chairs and such. Like overnight I learned the secret, involuntary handshake.

I made my way to my home office, sat in the captain's chair, and this is where you'll find me.

Kicking and screaming to be left alone by HD so I can have a productive existence.

# If I only had a brain . . .

October 11, 2015

I know that, as I write this, parts of my brain are dying. When I have bad headaches I always wonder if that is what it feels like to have brain cells die. But the cell death has been taking place over several years, before I had a clue.

So sometimes a headache is just a cigar.

My husband is out of town for a week. He is also known as my "Pre-frontal Cortex." He is the keeper of my working memory. My emotional barometer. The wall that separates me from not knowing, the frustration of not knowing, and the follow-through of every impulse. He is also the steadfast keeper of my heart.

Before he left, he told our ten-year old son to help me, and our son has really stepped up to the plate. He is a wonderful conversation partner. Last night, in an effort to cheer us both up from missing his dad, he asked me what my favorite movies were.

I drew a blank.

"It's not like that," I said. I can't just pull movie names out of the air anymore. If you showed me a list of movies, I could pick out the ones I love and tell you all about them."

"OK," he said, "A. What movies that start with A do you like?"

"That won't work either," I said. "If I hear the title I can tell you."

He was silent for a while and then he said,

"Mom, were you smart when you were a kid?"

"Why?" I asked.

"Did people think you were smart?"

"Actually, they did," I said.

"Did *you* think you were smart?" he asked.

"Well, yes. I thought I was smart. And I was smart. And I am still smart today, but there are some ways I can't think anymore."

I thought about the collections of muddled thoughts in my brain. The myriad of things that I can't keep sorted out. Things I need to ask other people to write down for me so I could post the explanations and look at them when I forget them five minutes later. And the fact that I don't know when to ask who what in order to get the kind of help I've just described. But I kept this part to myself. My son is very observant and insightful, and I know he has come to learn what my deficiencies are by just watching me try to function each day. But, last night, saying those facts out loud seemed like too much to say to a boy of ten who misses his father.

Instead, I asked him what his favorite movie was.

"Forrest Gump," he said. He watches it over and over on Netflix, he says, because each time he watches it, he picks up something he never noticed before.

The irony of his choice wasn't lost on me. I had to go look this up, but Forrest said that his mama always had a way of explaining things to him so that he could understand.

I am glad that I have people like Forrest's mom in my life. My husband. My friends. My kick-ass HD support team.

Still, I wonder what misunderstandings or forgettings will cause me to make mistakes or miss appointments or take things the wrong way this week, without my beloved and handsome Prefrontal Cortex.

It's going to be a long week, and maybe I'll learn something from the experience.

But if I do, I'd better make sure I write it down.

# Tripping over the yellow brick road

October 14, 2015

Days have passed since my husband left for the week. I think today is the middle day and he comes back Saturday.

I can't keep track of anything. I look over in the morning to talk to him when he is tying his shoes and he isn't there. I expect him to come home and he doesn't because he is 3000 miles away. Each time this happens, I relive the loss of remembering that he is far away. I oversleep every morning and forget to take my medicine or maybe take it twice.

The standards of hygiene and organization which formerly existed left this house when he did. I am unwashed, which is not so unusual. But this morning I washed my face with a washcloth that smelled like mildew and I couldn't take the smell, so I grabbed the first thing I could find to wipe it off my face. Unfortunately I grabbed the shirt that I have been wearing continuously and I rubbed the smelly armpit of it all over my face.

And I didn't know what to do next so I didn't do anything. My days now are sequences of not knowing what to do next. So that is how I set about my day:

With mildewy armpit face and unbrushed teeth.

My heart is gone now, as well as my brain. I miss my husband so much that his not being here has suspended the reality that existed before. The days are dragging by and, I am exhausted all of the time from trying to do all of the things that he usually does, which is mostly everything. I am living on junk food because I am too tired to cook.

I am sad because he is my favorite person and he is gone. I am stressed because when I trip over my own feet, I cannot complain to him about it. It feels like my skeleton has been ripped out.

But he is coming back in a few days and I hold onto that thought.

I am going to pull it together and try to make the house look nice again and even clean myself up.

I only have a few more steps until I get there. Until he gets here.

And I am so tired.

Tonight I was cooking over an extremely hot frying pan, and I felt it getting hotter and hotter, to the point where I thought the pan would catch on fire. Then I realized that my hand was down there in the heat, stirring the food. My broken intuition told me that the heat for the stove didn't apply to me, it was only for the stove, so I left my hand down there for a while longer. Then I decided it would be wise to turn the burner down and run cold water over my hand.

I've had a similar disconnect while driving. I'll wait and wait until it's my turn, and my turn never comes and I tell myself that the next car coming has nothing to do with me because I am finished with that part of waiting. And I pull out in front of the cars, and so far I have been lucky.

I try not to do that so much, especially when anyone is in the car with me.

But these kinds of things get my attention, and I'm glad they do.

I can fight an enemy I know about.

Already, alarm clocks are set for nearly every event in my day. My goal is to make it from bell to bell in one piece.

But, last time I checked, alarms and graphic organizers can't help with odd, almost purposeful, reckless behavior.

The implications of what I am doing or contemplating clicks into the action mode of my brain when it is almost too late to help myself.

So my next challenge is to try to, figuratively, run around and get in front of myself in risky situations. I know what some of them deal with: walking, showering, using stairs, getting out of bed, driving, food preparation and even dressing (I lost a battle with panty hose and landed on my butt.) I am going to try some sensory stimulation to put myself in the moment, and then take a few deep, relaxing breaths while I envision safe outcomes.

But I think the biggest help would be to if I could somehow ask myself what the hell I am doing before I do it.

I am not sure if I can do this, but I am going to try.

# Love to the rescue

I had been without my husband for nearly a week and had fallen apart.

He came home a day early.

He turned on the shower and told me to get in, and I stayed in there for about 30 minutes. Water is sharp and unpleasant when I am averse to it, but I stayed in there and made myself very clean. My husband got me out and gave me my pink fluffy robe to put on. Even though he was home, I was on a downhill path and needed to stop and turn it around. I explained to him that when he was gone, I felt empty and confused.

"Well," he said. "No more *me* going away. From now on it's *us*."

Later, we went to the movies and on the way out of the theater I fell into a wall.

"It's a first," I told him. "The first time I definitely seemed drunk in front of a crowd of people."

"It will be OK," he said. "I just need to walk closer to you so I can catch you." And he has.

Then at 5:00 this morning, I fell down the porch stairs in an effort to walk the toy poodle. I wasn't physically hurt but it felt like another first.

"It's OK," he said. "We'll get a longer leash, so you can stand on the porch while the dog goes in the yard."

The past few days, my motor control has declined dramatically. It feels like I walk like a scarecrow. I keep running into walls, counters, cabinets, and freezer doors. It is harder to type, to dress, and to do most everything.

In a moment of despair, after coming in for a landing on the couch, I looked at my husband and said, "I don't know what to do."

"I do," he said. "We'll roll with it."

And I believe him.

# Policing my own reckless behavior

Tonight I was cooking over an extremely hot frying pan, and I felt it getting hotter and hotter, to the point where I thought the pan would catch on fire. Then I realized that my hand was down there in the heat, stirring the food. My broken intuition told me that the heat for the stove didn't apply to me, it was only for the stove, so I left my hand down there for a while longer. Then I decided it would be wise to turn the burner down and run cold water over my hand.

I've had a similar disconnect while driving. I'll wait and wait until it's my turn, and my turn never comes and I tell myself that the next car coming has nothing to do with me because I am finished with that part of waiting. And I pull out in front of the cars, and so far I have been lucky.

I try not to do that so much, especially when anyone is in the car with me.

But these kinds of things get my attention, and I'm glad they do.

I can fight an enemy I know about.

Already, alarm clocks are set for nearly every event in my day. My goal is to make it from bell to bell in one piece.

But, last time I checked, alarms and graphic organizers can't help with odd, almost purposeful, reckless behavior.

The implications of what I am doing or contemplating clicks into the action mode of my brain when it is almost too late to help myself.

So my next challenge is to try to, figuratively, run around and get in front of myself in risky situations. I know what some of them deal with: walking, showering, using stairs, getting out of bed, driving, food preparation and even dressing (I lost a battle with panty hose and landed on my butt.) I am going to try some sensory stimulation to put myself in the moment, and then take a few deep, relaxing breaths while I envision safe outcomes.

But I think the biggest help would be to if I could somehow ask myself what the hell I am doing before I do it.

I am not sure if I can do this, but I am going to try.

# Having a big disease in a small town

November 10, 2015

Refusing to be that stereotypical HD lurker who watches life happen through curtains, I opened the door Saturday morning.

My husband, Randy, was out in the front yard with the leaf blower on. I was vaguely aware, as I engaged in some minor lurking activity from my station on the couch, that a man with a book had walked up to my husband, and was talking very loudly. My husband turned the leaf blower off and the man was still talking to him loudly.

That put me on high alert. I went to the door. The man had his back to me and was waving his hands in a way that I characterized as wildly. I thought he was part of a religious organization and that he was not going to ever, ever let Randy turn the leaf blower back on. I became really angry when I thought about the fact that my husband works very hard, takes care of the family, including me, and was just trying to get a little yard work done. He was probably tired.

That's when I stepped outside and said, "Excuse me sir!" or I could have said, "Hey you!

The man turned around with a big smile and I said firmly, "Please go away."

His smile faded, while at the same time my husband was saying, "This is a friend of mine. He is a former city alderman and he wanted to talk to me." Randy works at a newspaper.

My resolve crumbled and I backed up, back into the house, tripping over my own apologies, which still seem insufficient. The couch sucked me back into it and, my spirits too low to lurk, I cried a little bit. And then I wrote on Facebook, "I embarrassed myself in public again. Damn it."

You would think that in a town of 30,000 people, the details of what I had done would have evaporated on the street.

But by the end of the day, I was reached out to and reassured by a local radio show host and the former mayor. These gentlemen are, upstanding, genuine and kind as a rule. That they reached out did not surprise me. They are the kind of people who would stop what they were doing on a Saturday to tell me not to worry about what I did.

But what did surprise me was the speed with which the incident was spread around town. Once I was told, "It's none of your business what other people think about you," and I pretty much live by that rule. But I wondered how the story was relayed. Was my community alerting itself that I am getting worse? Do people pity me? Are they afraid of me?

There's no way to tell. But I live in a house without curtains and I'm not going to stop opening doors.

# My HD Affirmations

1.      I hate this disease and am going to fight against it with every fiber of my being.

2.      Today my primary plan and purpose is to kick the butt of HD.

3.      Today I will conquer HD.

4.      Today I choose to live as though I did not have HD.

5.      Today I reject HD in my life.

6.      Today I will step out from under the shadow of HD.

7.      Today I will not allow HD to haunt me.

8.      Today, in the fight against HD, I win.

9.      HD? Not today.

10.     Today I live without fear of HD.

11.     HD is not allowed in my life today.

12.     HD. I don't deny it: I defy it.

13.   Today I choose to focus on my (good) health and happiness.

14.   I release myself from the grip of HD today.

15.   Today HD can't get in my way.'

16.   Today I give myself permission to worry about HD TOMORROW.

17.   Today I choose to live in the HD-free zone.

18.   HD today? No way!

19.   Today, HD knocked me down but I got up and walked away.

20.   Today HD isn't stopping me.

21.   Today I will not let HD get the best of me.

22.   Today I choose to ignore HD.

23.   Today HD will not break my stride.

24.   Today HD is not me.

25.   Today I am a successful tightrope walker.

26.   Today I found joy in buying flat shoes.

27.   Today HD is a fact but not a specter.

28.   Today I have been too busy to worry about HD.

29.   Today I will forgive myself for being angry yesterday.

30.   Today I am grateful for my health and I am pulling for my friends who also have HD.

31.   Today I will sidestep HD.

32.   Today HD will stand in the corner while I get some stuff done.

33.   Today I will pray for relief for other families suffering from HD.

34.   Today I am grateful for all of the research going on.

35.   Today HD will not take center stage.

36.   Today I will persevere despite HD.

37.   _on't you know t_at one _appy _ay
we and our c_il_ren will not  _ave to live wit_ it?
T_ere will be a cure!

38.   Today I am walking towards a cure
for HD.

39.   Today HD will not take or break my
spirit.

40.   Today I will work on local HD
advocacy.

41.   HD is not the boss of me today.